First World War

and Army of Occupation

War Diary

France, Belgium and Germany

32 DIVISION
97 Infantry Brigade,
Brigade Machine Gun Company
4 March 1916 - 21 February 1918

WO95/2404/4

The Naval & Military Press Ltd
www.nmarchive.com
Published in association with The National Archives

Published by

The Naval & Military Press Ltd

Unit 10 Ridgewood Industrial Park,

Uckfield, East Sussex,

TN22 5QE England

Tel: +44 (0) 1825 749494

www.naval-military-press.com

www.nmarchive.com

This diary has been reprinted in facsimile from the original. Any imperfections are inevitably reproduced and the quality may fall short of modern type and cartographic standards.

Contents

Document type	Place/Title	Date From	Date To
Heading	WO95/2404/4		
Heading	32nd Division 97th Infy Bde 97th Mach Gun Coy Mar 1916-Feb 1918		
Heading	97th Brigade 32nd Division Disembarked Havre From U.K 11.3.16 97th Brigade Machine Gun Company March 1916		
Miscellaneous	DAAG C11 Passed Sent Died to this Office.	02/05/1916	02/05/1916
War Diary	Grantham	10/03/1916	10/03/1916
War Diary	Havre	12/03/1916	12/03/1916
War Diary	Albert	16/03/1916	31/03/1916
Heading	97th Brigade 32nd Division 97th Brigade Machine Gun Company April 1916		
Heading	War Diary Of 97th Machine Gun Company From 1st April 1916 To 30th April 1916	01/05/1916	01/05/1916
War Diary	Albert	01/04/1916	03/04/1916
War Diary	Warloy	04/03/1916	12/04/1916
War Diary	Bouzincourt	13/04/1916	24/04/1916
War Diary	Warloy	25/04/1916	30/04/1916
Heading	97th Brigade 32nd Division 97th Brigade Machine Gun Company May 1916		
Heading	War Diary Of 97th Brigade Machine Gun Company From 1st May 1916 To 31st May 1916		
War Diary	Warloy	01/05/1916	05/05/1916
War Diary	Contay	06/05/1916	17/05/1916
War Diary	Warloy	18/05/1916	18/05/1916
War Diary	Bouzincourt	19/05/1916	31/05/1916
Diagram etc	Appendix I		
Heading	97th Brigade 32nd Division 97th Brigade Machine Gun Company		
Heading	War Diary Of 97th Brigade Machine Gun Coy From 1st June 1916 To 30th June 1916 Vol 4		
War Diary	Warloy	01/06/1916	12/06/1916
War Diary	Contay	13/06/1916	22/06/1916
War Diary	Bouzincourt	23/06/1916	23/06/1916
War Diary	Authville	24/06/1916	30/06/1916
Heading	War Diary 97th Machine Gun Company July 1916		
Heading	War Diary Of The 97th Machine Gun Company Evening The Period. July 1st 1916 To July 31st 1916	31/07/1916	31/07/1916
War Diary	Authville	01/07/1916	02/07/1916
War Diary		01/07/1916	03/07/1916
War Diary	Authville	01/07/1916	02/07/1916
War Diary	Authville	01/07/1916	01/07/1916
War Diary	Authville	03/07/1916	03/07/1916
War Diary	Aveluy	03/07/1916	03/07/1916
War Diary	Warloy	04/07/1916	05/07/1916
War Diary	Harponville	06/07/1916	07/07/1916
War Diary	Senlis	08/07/1916	08/07/1916
War Diary	Ovilliers Sector	09/07/1916	15/07/1916
War Diary	Bouzincourt	16/07/1916	16/07/1916
War Diary	Amplier	17/07/1916	17/07/1916

War Diary	Sus St Leger	18/07/1916	19/07/1916
War Diary	Tachincourt	20/07/1916	20/07/1916
War Diary	Huclier	21/07/1916	21/07/1916
War Diary	Allouagne	22/07/1916	26/07/1916
War Diary	Bethune	27/07/1916	31/07/1916
Heading	97th Brigade 32nd Division 97th Brigade Machine Gun Company August 1916		
Heading	War Diary Of 97th Machine Gun Company For The Month Of August 1916 From 1st August 1916 To 31st August 1916 Vol 6		
War Diary	Bethune	01/08/1916	05/08/1916
War Diary	Cambrin	05/08/1916	30/08/1916
War Diary	Bethune	31/08/1916	31/08/1916
Heading	97th Brigade 32nd Division 97th Brigade Machine Gun Company September 1916		
Heading	97th Machine Gun Company Original War Diary Volume VII For September 1916		
Miscellaneous	Headquarters 97th Infantry Brigade Herewith Vol VII Original War Diary For Month Of September 1916	30/09/1916	30/09/1916
War Diary	Bethune	01/09/1916	06/09/1916
War Diary	Le Preol (Cuinchy)	07/09/1916	08/09/1916
War Diary	Cuinchy Sector	09/09/1916	25/09/1916
War Diary	Bethune	26/09/1916	30/09/1916
Miscellaneous	Appendix A List Of Targets	30/09/1916	30/09/1916
Map			
Heading	97th Brigade 32nd Division 97th Brigade Machine Gun Company October 1916		
Heading	War Diary of 97th Machine Gun Company To The Month Of October 1916 Volume VIII		
War Diary	Bethune	01/10/1916	02/10/1916
War Diary	Cambrin	03/10/1916	12/10/1916
War Diary	Bethune	13/10/1916	14/10/1916
War Diary	Labeuvriere	15/10/1916	15/10/1916
War Diary	La Thieuloye	16/10/1916	16/10/1916
War Diary	Sericourt	17/10/1916	17/10/1916
War Diary	Longvillette	18/10/1916	20/10/1916
War Diary	Rubempre	21/10/1916	22/10/1916
War Diary	Bouzincourt	23/10/1916	29/10/1916
War Diary	Rubempre	30/10/1916	30/10/1916
War Diary	Val-De-Maison	31/10/1916	31/10/1916
Heading	97th Brigade 32nd Division 97th Brigade Machine Gun Company November 1916		
Heading	War Diary Of 97th Machine Gun Company For The Month Of November 1916 Volume No IX	30/11/1916	30/11/1916
War Diary	Val-De-Maison	01/11/1916	12/11/1916
War Diary	Contay	13/11/1916	13/11/1916
War Diary	Martinsart	14/11/1916	14/11/1916
War Diary	Englebelmer	15/11/1916	16/11/1916
War Diary	Trenches. W Of Beaumont-Hamel	17/11/1916	18/11/1916
War Diary	Englebelmer	19/11/1916	20/11/1916
War Diary	Mailly-Maillet	21/11/1916	22/11/1916
War Diary	Raincheval	23/11/1916	24/11/1916
War Diary	Beauval	25/11/1916	25/11/1916
War Diary	Berteaucourt	26/11/1916	30/11/1916

Miscellaneous	Appendix to Entries Dated 17/11/16 18/11/16 19/11/16 Action of Company Operation in Above Dates Action of No 1 Section.		
Miscellaneous	Action Of No. 2 Section		
Miscellaneous	Action Of No 3 Section		
Miscellaneous	Action Of No 4 Section		
Heading	97th Brigade 32nd Division 97th Brigade Machine Gun Company December 1916		
Heading	97th Machine Gun Company War Diary For Month Of December Volume X	02/01/1917	02/01/1917
War Diary	Berteaucourt	01/12/1916	15/12/1916
War Diary	Rubempre	16/12/1916	31/12/1916
Heading	97th M.G. Coy. War Diary For Month Of January 1917 Volume XI	31/01/1917	31/01/1917
War Diary	Rubempre	01/01/1917	05/01/1917
War Diary	Courcelle	06/01/1917	15/01/1917
War Diary	Bus-En-Artois	16/01/1917	19/01/1917
War Diary	Beaumont-Hamel	20/01/1917	31/01/1917
Heading	97th Machine Gun Coy Originals War Diary For February 1917 Volume XII	28/02/1916	28/02/1916
War Diary	Beamont-Hamel	01/02/1917	17/02/1917
War Diary	Harponville	18/02/1917	18/02/1917
War Diary	Vadencourt	19/02/1917	20/02/1917
War Diary	St Acheul	21/02/1917	21/02/1917
War Diary	Aubercourt	22/02/1917	24/02/1917
War Diary	Beaucourt	25/02/1917	28/02/1917
Miscellaneous	Appendix To Entry Dated 10/2/17 Action Of 97th M.G. Coy. During		
Miscellaneous			
Miscellaneous	Action Of No. 3 Section		
Miscellaneous			
Miscellaneous	Action Of No 4 Section		
Miscellaneous	Headquarters 97th Inf Bde	31/03/1917	31/03/1917
Heading	97th Machine Gun Coy Original War Diary For Month Of March 1917 Volume XIII		
War Diary	Beaucourt En Santerre	01/03/1917	02/03/1917
War Diary	Rouvroy	03/03/1917	15/03/1917
War Diary	Mezieres	16/03/1917	16/03/1917
War Diary	Beaufort Wood	17/03/1917	17/03/1917
War Diary	La Chavatte	18/03/1917	18/03/1917
War Diary	Herly	19/03/1917	19/03/1917
War Diary	Nesle	20/03/1917	27/03/1917
War Diary	Foreste	28/03/1917	31/03/1917
Heading	97th M G Coy War Diary For Month Of April 1917 Volume XIII	30/04/1917	30/04/1917
War Diary	Savy	01/04/1917	15/04/1917
War Diary	Foreste	16/04/1917	19/04/1917
War Diary	Hombleux	20/04/1917	24/04/1917
War Diary	Offoy	26/04/1917	30/04/1917
Heading	97th M G Coy War Diary For May 1917 Volume XV	30/05/1917	30/05/1917
War Diary		01/05/1917	31/05/1917
Miscellaneous	War Diary For Month Of June Vol XI		
War Diary	Doulieu Area	01/06/1917	13/06/1917
War Diary	Dunkerque Area	14/06/1917	16/06/1917
War Diary	Coxyde De Area	18/06/1917	26/06/1917
War Diary	Nieuport	27/06/1917	30/06/1917

Miscellaneous Heading	97th M.G Coy War Diary For July 1917 Volume XII		
Miscellaneous Heading	97th M.G Coy War Diary For August 1917 Volume XIII		
War Diary	Coxyde	01/08/1917	14/08/1917
War Diary	Bray Dunes	15/08/1917	17/08/1917
War Diary	Ghyvelde	18/08/1917	27/08/1917
War Diary	S.Georges Sector	28/08/1917	31/08/1917
Heading	97th M.G Coy War Diary For Month Of September 1917 Volume XIV		
War Diary	Right Sub-Sector Nieuport Sector	01/09/1917	21/09/1917
War Diary	Coxyde	21/09/1917	21/09/1917
War Diary	Bray-Dunes Plage	22/09/1917	24/09/1917
War Diary	Coxyde	24/09/1917	29/09/1917
War Diary	Left Sub-Sector Nieuport Sector	29/09/1917	30/09/1917
War Diary	Lombartzyde Subsector	01/10/1917	05/10/1917
War Diary	Coxyde	06/10/1917	06/10/1917
War Diary	Uxem	07/10/1917	23/10/1917
War Diary	Rubrouck	25/10/1917	31/10/1917
Heading	97th M.G Coy War Diary For Month Of October 1917 Volume XV		
Heading	97th M.G Coy War Diary For Month Of November 1917 Volume XVI		
War Diary	Rubruck	01/11/1917	09/11/1917
War Diary	Wormhoudt	10/11/1917	10/11/1917
War Diary	Road Camp Poperinghe	11/11/1917	21/11/1917
War Diary	Irish Farm	22/11/1917	24/11/1917
War Diary	Canal Bank	25/11/1917	30/11/1917
War Diary	Irish Farm	01/12/1917	03/12/1917
War Diary	Dambre Camp	04/12/1917	15/12/1917
War Diary	Canal Bank	16/12/1917	17/12/1917
War Diary	Hubner F.M.	18/12/1917	24/12/1917
War Diary	Siege Camp	25/12/1917	30/12/1917
War Diary	Autingues	31/12/1917	31/12/1917
Heading	War Diary Of 97th M.G. Company From 1st Jan 1918 To 31st Dec 1918 Vol 23		
War Diary	Autingues	01/01/1918	12/01/1918
War Diary	Zouafques	13/01/1918	17/01/1918
War Diary	Nordasques	18/01/1918	19/01/1918
War Diary	G Camp	20/01/1918	24/01/1918
War Diary	Cyrille Van Damme	25/01/1918	27/01/1918
War Diary	Mondovi Wood	28/01/1918	31/01/1918
Heading	War Diary Of 97th M.G. Company For Period-1st February To 21st February 1918 Vol 24		
War Diary	Mondovi Wood	01/02/1918	01/02/1918
War Diary	Astor Camp	02/02/1918	04/02/1918
War Diary	Mondovi Wood	05/02/1918	21/02/1918
Operation(al) Order(s)	97th Machine Gun Company Operation Order No 35 Appendix "A"		
Operation(al) Order(s)	97th Machine Gun Coy Operation Order No 37 Appendix "B"	10/02/1918	10/02/1918
Operation(al) Order(s)	97th Machine Gun Coy Operation Order No 38 Appendix "C"	13/02/1918	13/02/1918
Operation(al) Order(s)	97th Machine Gun Company Operation Order No 40 Appendix "D"	18/02/1918	18/02/1918

Operation(al) Order(s)	97th Machine Gun Company Operation Order No 41 Appendix "E"	19/02/1918	19/02/1918
Miscellaneous	Operation Orders 14th Company Machine Gun Corps No. 43	19/02/1918	19/02/1918
Miscellaneous	March Table "A" To Company 97th Inf. Bde.		
Miscellaneous	Table "B" To Accompany 97th. Inf. Bde. O.O. 204		
Operation(al) Order(s)	97th Infantry Brigade Operation Order No 204	13/02/1918	13/02/1918

32ND DIVISION
97TH INFY BDE

97TH MACH GUN COY
MAR 1916- FEB 1918

97th Brigade.

32nd Division.

Disembarked Havre from U.K. 11.3.16.

97th BRIGADE MACHINE GUN COMPANY

MARCH 1 9 1 6;

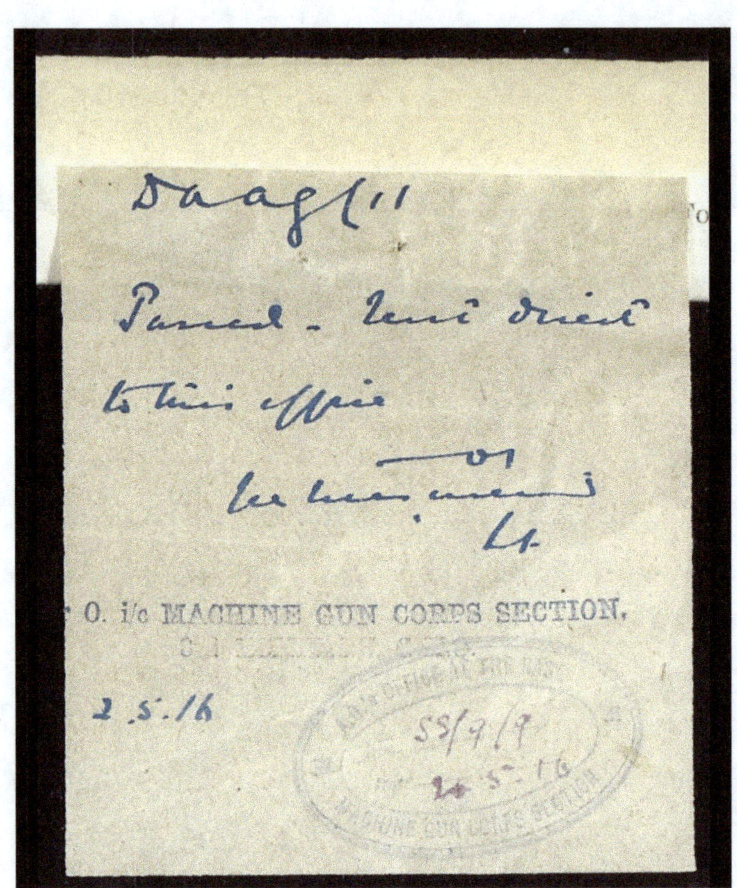

DAAG (1)

Passed – sent direct to this office

[illegible]

Lt

O. i/c MACHINE GUN CORPS SECTION.

2.5.16

55/9/9

24-5-16

Instructions regarding War Diaries and Intelligence Summaries are contained in F. S. Regs., Part II. and the Staff Manual respectively. Title pages will be prepared in manuscript.

WAR DIARY
or
~~INTELLIGENCE SUMMARY.~~
(Erase heading not required.)

Form C. 2118.

Place	Date	Hour	Summary of Events and Information	Remarks and references to Appendices
	1916			
Grantham	Mar 10	6.00am.	The Company left BELTON PARK CAMP, GRANTHAM, at 6.00 am. on Friday, March 10th, 1916, having been delayed for two and a half hours by some of the mules breaking loose in a snow storm. A ten minutes halt was made in GRANTHAM for coffee, kindly provided by Countess Brownlow. The Company arrived at the Military Siding at GRANTHAM STATION at 8.15 am. and was entrained in a quarter of an hour. The train left at 8.45 am. and reached SOUTHAMPTON DOCKS at 5.15 pm., the only stop being for half an hour at HOLLOWAY STATION, LONDON, where the horses were watered. A party of six officers and 50 men, under LIEUT. C. S. SMITH, embarked on the transport "MONA'S QUEEN", while the remainder of the company, with the company transport, embarked on the transport "DUSKY MILLER". The Veterinary Officer at SOUTHAMPTON exchanged one horse and two mules, on account of lameness caused by cracked heels due to exposure in mud at GRANTHAM for two weeks. LIEUT. SMITH'S party left SOUTHAMPTON	

T2134. Wt. W708—776. 500000. 4/15. Sir J. C. & S.

Instructions regarding War Diaries and Intelligence Summaries are contained in F. S. Regs., Part II. and the Staff Manual respectively. Title pages will be prepared in manuscript.

WAR DIARY

or

~~INTELLIGENCE SUMMARY.~~

(Erase heading not required.)

Army Form C. 2118.

Place	Date 1916	Hour	Summary of Events and Information	Remarks and references to Appendices
			at 7.30 p.m. and reached HAVRE without incident, where it disembarked at 7.30 a.m. on Saturday, 11th March. It marched to No 2 CAMP, SANVIC, HAVRE and was accomodated in tents. The remainder of the company left SOUTHAMPTON at 7.30 p.m. and disembarked at HAVRE at midday and joined LIEUT. SMITH'S party at No. 2 CAMP. The transport was picketed in the open.	
HAVRE	Mar 12		At 9.00 a.m. on Sunday, March 12th, an inspection was held by the Camp Commandant, and a list of deficiencies in equipment made. These deficiences were drawn from the Ordnance and distributed on Monday, March 13th. At 6.00 a.m. on Tuesday, March 14th, the company left No. 2 CAMP and entrained at the GARE DES MARCHANDISES, HAVRE at 8.30 a.m., occupying the same train as the 96th. MACHINE GUN COMPANY. The company travelled by train via ROUEN and AMIENS to railhead at MERICOURT, which was reached at 10.00 p.m. on the same day. The company detrained at once and marched to	

T2134. Wt. W708-776. 500000. 4/15. Sir J. C. & S.

Instructions regarding War Diaries and Intelligence Summaries are contained in F. S. Regs., Part II. and the Staff Manual respectively. Title pages will be prepared in manuscript.

WAR DIARY
or
~~INTELLIGENCE SUMMARY.~~
(Erase heading not required.)

Army Form C. 2118.

Place	Date 1916	Hour	Summary of Events and Information	Remarks and references to Appendices
			DERNANCOURT, where it was billeted for the rest of the night in barns. At 2.00 pm. on Wednesday, March 15th. the company left DERNANCOURT for ALBERT, having been preceded by a billeting party, and there went into billets in empty private residences in the RUE DE BAPAUME, the transport being placed in a disused factory in RUE HURTU. From the day the company landed in FRANCE the weather has been bright and warm.	
ALBERT	Mar 16.		On Thursday morning, Mar 16th. a party, consisting of LIEUTS. SMITH + WALLACE, 4 N.C.O's and 12 men, went into the trenches joining up with the 15th MOTOR MACHINE GUN BATTERY occupying sectors E1 + E2, belonging to the 97th BRIGADE. On Friday, March 17th. the company went for a route march to HEDAUVILLE under 2nd LIEUT. ELLISTON. On Saturday, March 18th. a party consisting of 2nd LIEUTS. ELLISTON and HANNAH, 4 N.C.O's and 12 men relieved the party already in the trenches, which party was in turn relieved by a similar party under 2nd LIEUTS. LAVENDER and	

T2134. Wt. W708—776. 500000. 4/15. Sir J. C. & S.

Army Form C. 2118.

WAR DIARY
or
INTELLIGENCE SUMMARY.
(Erase heading not required.)

Instructions regarding War Diaries and Intelligence Summaries are contained in F. S. Regs., Part II. and the Staff Manual respectively. Title pages will be prepared in manuscript.

Place	Date 1916	Hour	Summary of Events and Information	Remarks and references to Appendices
			JINKS on Monday, March 20th. On Tuesday, March 21st, the transport was removed to DERNANCOURT on account of the constant shelling of ALBERT by the enemy, the guns and stores from the limber wagons being placed in the cellars under the houses occupied by the various sections. On Wednesday, March 22nd. a party under 2nd LIEUTS. CRAVEN and POWNALL relieved the party in the trenches. During the days March 18th to March 23rd. digging parties went into the trenches to construct new machine gun emplacements and dug-outs; while other parties dug trenches in the gardens behind the houses for occupation during bombardment.	
ALBERT	Mar 23.		On Thursday, March 23, the company took over the whole front of sectors E1 & E2 from the 15th MOTOR MACHINE GUN BATTERY, sections 3 and 4 being in the trenches, with four guns. The day passed quietly.	
ALBERT	Mar 24.		During the day work was continued on the two dugouts in MONIKIE STREET and DUNDEE AVENUE. At 8.00 p.m. 2nd LIEUT. CRAVEN	

T2134. Wt. W708—776. 500000. 4/15. Sir J. C. & S.

Instructions regarding War Diaries and Intelligence Summaries are contained in F. S. Regs., Part II. and the Staff Manual respectively. Title pages will be prepared in manuscript.

WAR DIARY
or
~~INTELLIGENCE SUMMARY.~~
(Erase heading not required.)

Army Form C. 2118.

Place	Date 1916	Hour	Summary of Events and Information	Remarks and references to Appendices
ALBERT	Mar. 24.		in conjunction with Trench Mortar Batteries, bombarded LABOISELLE with two guns. During the night the two guns under 2nd LIEUT. POWNALL fired at point Y025, (Ref. Map. 57D S.E. 4. Second edition) in X 20 d.	
	Mar. 25.		Work on the two dugouts was continued as on the previous day. At night the gun in the HERAULT STREET emplacement fired bursts at two points, where the enemy barbed wire was cut by our artillery during the afternoon, near the mine craters (Ref. Map 57D. S.E. 4. Second edition, square X 13 d), in order to prevent it being repaired. The gun in the ~~Arbroath~~ ARBROATH STREET emplacement fired during the night at the cross roads behind LABOISELLE (Ref. Map 57D. S.E. 4. Second edition, in square X 14 c).	
	Mar. 26.		At 3.00 p.m. Sections 3 + 4 were relieved by Sections 1 + 2 under LIEUT. SMITH and 2nd LIEUT. ELLISTON respectively, three guns belonging to each section being taken. From 8.00 p.m. till 10.00 p.m. the gun in HERAULT STREET fired on the barbed wire as on the previous day, and one gun in BON ACCORD STREET at point Y025 as on 24th. inst.	

Army Form C. 2118.

WAR DIARY
or
~~INTELLIGENCE SUMMARY.~~
(Erase heading not required.)

Instructions regarding War Diaries and Intelligence Summaries are contained in F. S. Regs., Part II. and the Staff Manual respectively. Title pages will be prepared in manuscript.

Place	Date 1916	Hour	Summary of Events and Information	Remarks and references to Appendices
ALBERT	Nov. 27th.		At 1.27 am. a mine near LA BOISELLE was exploded, which was a signal for a raiding party of the 2nd. DORSETS to make a raid on THE NOSE at LA BOISELLE (Ref. Map. 57D. S.E. 4. Second edition, in square X13d.) Guns were mounted in HERAULT STREET and two in ARBROATH STREET to fire at the LA BOISELLE communication trenches, while the artillery made a barrage all round THE NOSE. The two guns of No 1. Section in BON ACCORD STREET also fired to their direct front. The retaliatory bombardment which followed the raid was the first heavy fire to which the company had been subjected, and the way in which the gunners in HERAULT STREET and the open emplacements in ARBROATH STREET stuck to their work was highly creditable. During the day work was continued on the MONIKIE STREET dugout and emplacement by working parties of Nos. 3 + 4 Sections. From 7.30 pm till 8.30 pm the HERAULT STREET gun fired on the barbed wire as previously. LIEUT. WALLACE was admitted to hospital with influenza. The state of the trenches was much improved with drier weather.	

T2134. Wt. W708–776. 500000. 4/15. Sir J. C. & S.

Army Form C. 2118.

Instructions regarding War Diaries and Intelligence Summaries are contained in F. S. Regs., Part II. and the Staff Manual respectively. Title pages will be prepared in manuscript.

WAR DIARY
or
~~INTELLIGENCE SUMMARY.~~
(Erase heading not required.)

Place	Date 1916	Hour	Summary of Events and Information	Remarks and references to Appendices
ALBERT	Mar. 28th.		During the day and night work was carried on at the MONIKIE STREET and DUNDEE AVENUE dug outs and the MONIKIE STREET emplacement completed. 2nd LIEUT. POWNALL was admitted to hospital at WARLOY with bronchitis. From 7.30 to 8.30 pm. a gun in ARBROATH STREET fired at the cross roads as on 25th. inst. and the HERAULT STREET gun fired short bursts at frequent intervals during the night at the barbed wire as previously. During the night the emplacements in BON ACCORD STREET received much needed strengthening + overhead cover.	
	Mar. 29.		Work was continued on the MONIKIE STREET and DUNDEE AVENUE dugouts. At night the HERAULT STREET and ARBROATH STREET guns fired as on the preceeding day, while the right hand gun in BON ACCORD STREET fired indirect on LOZENGE WOOD (Ref. Map 57.D. SE.4, second edition, square X 27 b.) at frequent intervals during the night. The weather was bright and warm during the day, but rather cold at night.	
	Mar. 30.		At 3.00 pm. Sections 3 + 4 under 2nd LIEUTS. CRAVEN and HANNAH respectively relieved sections 1 + 2. Firing was carried out as on the	

T2134. Wt. W708-776. 500000. 4/15. Sir J. C. & S.

Instructions regarding War Diaries and Intelligence Summaries are contained in F. S. Regs., Part II. and the Staff Manual respectively. Title pages will be prepared in manuscript.

WAR DIARY

or

~~INTELLIGENCE SUMMARY.~~

(Erase heading not required.)

Army Form C. 2118.

Place	Date 1916	Hour	Summary of Events and Information	Remarks and references to Appendices
ALBERT	Mar. 30th.		previous day.	
	Mar. 31st.		A class of 12 men, consisting of 3 men from each of the four battalions in the 97th Brigade, commenced a course of instruction in the machine gun under SGT.-MAJOR SAVAGE, with a view to replacing casualties in or augmenting the strength of the company. Work on the dugouts and firing at night were continued as on the previous day. A working party under 2nd LIEUT. ELLISTON during the night built a battle emplacement at point 6095 in square X 19c, and also repaired an old one about 100 yards south of that point in ~~Dalhousie~~ DALHOUSIE STREET. These were made with a view to covering the enemy's trenches between points 3465 ~~and~~ in square X 20 a and 4330 in square X 20 b.	
			Eric S. Elliston, 2nd Lt.	

T2134. Wt. W708—776. 500000. 4/15. Sir J. C. & S.

97th Brigade.

32nd Division.

97th BRIGADE. MACHINE GUN COMPANY

APRIL 1 9 1 6

3280 ii

Confidential

Vol 2

War Diary of

97th Machine Gun Company

from 1st April 1916 to 30th April 1916.

W. W. Stanley Capt
O.C. 97th Bde M G Coy

1-5-16

Instructions regarding War Diaries and Intelligence Summaries are contained in F. S. Regs., Part II. and the Staff Manual respectively. Title pages will be prepared in manuscript.

WAR DIARY
or
~~INTELLIGENCE SUMMARY.~~
(Erase heading not required.)

Army Form C. 2118.

Place	Date 1916	Hour	Summary of Events and Information	Remarks and references to Appendices
ALBERT	Apr. 1st.		Work was continued in the trenches as on the previous days. During the night another emplacement with overhead cover was made in DUNDEE AVENUE to the east of ARBROATH STREET with a view to replacing the open emplacement in ARBROATH STREET for firing on LA BOISELLE village. This was under the direction of 2nd LIEUT. CRAVEN. An inspection of the transport at DERNANCOURT was held during the morning by a member of the BRIGADIER-GENERAL'S staff. Weather continuing fine.	
	Apr. 2nd.		A gun team from each of sections 1 + 2 under LIEUT. SMITH and 2nd LIEUT. ELLISTON respectively augmented the strength in the trenches with a view to assisting a raiding party during the evening. The disposition of guns was as follows:- 2 guns in HERAULT STREET and ARBROATH STREET under 2nd LIEUT. ELLISTON; 2 guns in DUNDEE AVENUE and MONIKIE STREET under 2nd LIEUT. CRAVEN; 2 guns in BON ACCORD STREET under LIEUT. SMITH. The first three guns were to fire at and to the right of LA BOISELLE, the fourth gun at point 7925 in	

T2131. Wt. W708—776. 500000. 4/15. Sir J. C. & S.

Instructions regarding War Diaries and Intelligence Summaries are contained in F. S. Regs., Part II. and the Staff Manual respectively. Title pages will be prepared in manuscript.

~~INTELLIGENCE SUMMARY~~

WAR DIARY

or

~~INTELLIGENCE SUMMARY.~~

(Erase heading not required.)

Army Form C. 2118.

Place	Date 1916	Hour	Summary of Events and Information	Remarks and references to Appendices
ALBERT	Apr. 2nd.		square X 26 b and the remaining two at point 8192 in square X 20d. All to open fire at a prearranged signal. Two guns were kept in reserve at BECOURT CHATEAU in square X 25d under 2nd LIEUT. HANNAH.	
	Apr. 3rd.		The prearranged signal was to have been the firing of a torpedo, "soon after 1.00 am" but owing to the lightness of the night the operations were cancelled at 2.30 am. The raid was to have been carried out against the trenches near point 7025 in square X 20d. by the 17th H.L.I. in conjunction with the 11th. BORDER REGT. The rest of the day was mostly spent in packing up and preparing to leave ALBERT on the following day.	
WARLOY	Apr. 4th.		A billeting party under 2nd LIEUT. ELLISTON left ALBERT at 6.45 am for WARLOY (Ref. Map, France, No 11, LENS, square 6G). Sections 1 + 2 followed with full transport at 10.00 and 11.00 am respectively. Sections 3 and 4 followed at 5.00 pm, having been relieved in the trenches at 2.00 pm. by the 23rd Machine Gun Company in E1 Sector and the	

Instructions regarding War Diaries and Intelligence Summaries are contained in F. S. Regs., Part II. and the Staff Manual respectively. Title pages will be prepared in manuscript.

WAR DIARY
or
~~INTELLIGENCE SUMMARY.~~
(Erase heading not required.)

Army Form C. 2118.

Place	Date 1916	Hour	Summary of Events and Information	Remarks and references to Appendices
WARLOY	Apr 4th.		63rd MACHINE GUN COMPANY in E2 sector. The billets were found to compare very unfavourably with those just vacated in ALBERT, being very cramped and nothing but barns without bunks. The whole village of WARLOY was packed to its very fullest extent.	
	Apr. 5th		The day was spent cleaning up billets, thoroughly overhauling the guns and digging latrines, &c. The following reinforcements arrived:– Pte. BURTON, A. No. 12400. " BARTON, W. " 7534.	
	Apr. 6th		The company paraded in sections from 9.30 am to 12.30 pm for rifle and squad drill and inspection of arms and equipment.	
	Apr. 7th		The company paraded in sections from 9.30 am to 12.30 pm and from 2.30 pm to 4.00 pm for drill + mechanism. In the afternoon 2nd LIEUTS. ELLISTON and LAVENDER proceeded to SENLIS (same reference) to attend a lecture on "Gas", but, owing to the tardiness of the motor lorry ordered for them by the Brigade, only got to the lecture five minutes before its conclusion. LIEUT. SMITH was taken to the	

T2134. Wt. W708—776. 500000. 4/15. Sir J. C. & S.

Army Form C. 2118.

Instructions regarding War Diaries and Intelligence Summaries are contained in F. S. Regs., Part II. and the Staff Manual respectively. Title pages will be prepared in manuscript.

or

~~INTELLIGENCE SUMMARY.~~

(*Erase heading not required.*)

Place	Date 1916	Hour	Summary of Events and Information	Remarks and references to Appendices
WARLOY	Apr. 7th.		CASUALTY CLEARING STATION, having contracted German measles.	
	Apr. 8th.		The company was inspected by BRIGADIER-GENERAL J.B. JARDINE at 10.00 a.m. The inspection was followed by kit adjustment.	
	Apr. 9th.		The weather was fine and warm. LIEUT. WALLACE and 2nd LIEUT. POWNALL were discharged from hospital & rejoined the Coy.	
	Apr. 10th.		At 2.00 p.m. Nos. 2 + 4 Sections, under LIEUT. E.L. WALLACE, proceeded to AVELUY via MILLENCOURT and ALBERT (Ref. Map, France, No11, LENS, square 6 H) to take over from the 14th. MACHINE GUN COMPANY and to improve the defences of the village.	
	Apr. 11th.		The party under LIEUT. WALLACE commenced the improvement of the machine gun emplacements in AVELUY. The village was heavily shelled during the evening, when the men were ordered to the cellars below their billets; the cellars were found to be quite inadequate for the number of men billetted.	
	Apr. 12th.		At 12.30 p.m. the company relieved the 14th MACHINE GUN COMPANY in the trenches in Sector G1, AVELUY to AUTHUILLE, (Ref. Map,	

T2131. Wt. W708–776. 500000. 4/15. Sir J. C. & S.

Instructions regarding War Diaries and Intelligence Summaries are contained in F. S. Regs., Part II. and the Staff Manual respectively. Title pages will be prepared in manuscript.

WAR DIARY
or
~~INTELLIGENCE SUMMARY.~~
(Erase heading not required.)

Army Form C. 2118.

Place	Date 1916	Hour	Summary of Events and Information	Remarks and references to Appendices
WARLOY	Apr.	12th.	France, sheet 57D, S.E., edition 2). The disposition of the guns was as follows:-	
			Under 2nd LIEUT. CRAVEN. One gun in front line trenches near CHOWBENT STREET; one gun in TOBERMORY STREET; two guns in AUTHUILLE; and one gun in reserve.	
			Under 2nd. LIEUT. ELLISTON. Two guns in AUTHUILLE WOOD; one gun in CHECQUERBENT STREET; and one gun in BURY AVENUE.	
			Under 2nd. LIEUT. HANNAH. One gun at WOOD POST; and one gun in reserve.	
			Under 2nd LIEUT. POWNALL. Four guns for the BRIDGE HEAD defences	
			One gun to be retained at BOUZINCOURT for instructional purposes. The guns disposed of as above were for purely defensive work. The relief was carried out under a steady downpour of rain. Company headquarters was established at BOUZINCOURT (Ref. Map, France, X011, LENS, square 6 H).	

Instructions regarding War Diaries and Intelligence Summaries are contained in F. S. Regs., Part II. and the Staff Manual respectively. Title pages will be prepared in manuscript.

~~WAR DIARY~~
or
INTELLIGENCE SUMMARY.
(*Erase heading not required.*)

Place	Date 1916	Hour	Summary of Events and Information	Remarks and references to Appendices
BOUZINCOURT	Apr.	13th.	The only firing done was by one of the BRIDGEHEAD defence guns, which fired intermittently all night at OVILLERS (Ref. Map, France, sheet 57D, S.E. edition 2, square X 8.).	
	Apr.	14th.	The BRIDGE HEAD gun fired as on the previous day. The gun kept in reserve under 2nd LIEUT. CRAVEN was transferred to AUTHUILLE WOOD under 2nd LIEUT. ELLISTON, and fired intermittently from 8.00 till 10.00 pm at the enemy second line trenches round about point 68, (Ref. Map, France, sheet 57D, S.E., edition 2, square R31c.). The company sustained its first casualty at 7.30 pm.; PTE. LANE, W.G., was hit by a stray bullet while carrying rations.	
	Apr.	15th	Firing was continued as on the previous day by the two guns. Weather bright & warm. {G.S. Limber Wagon and 2 draught horses with Driver Cragg, A.S.C. joined Divisional Train at VADENCOURT.	
	Apr.	16th	Firing was continued as on the previous day.	
	Apr.	17th	Firing was continued as on the previous day, except that the gun in ~~In~~ AUTHUILLE WOOD kept on until 11.00 pm. The gun under 2nd Lt. CRAVEN in the front line trenches was withdrawn and	

Instructions regarding War Diaries and Intelligence Summaries are contained in F. S. Regs., Part II. and the Staff Manual respectively. Title pages will be prepared in manuscript.

or

~~INTELLIGENCE~~ SUMMARY.

(*Erase heading not required.*)

Place	Date 1916	Hour	Summary of Events and Information	Remarks and references to Appendices
BOUZINCOURT	Apr. 17th		Held in reserve. Steady rain all day.	
	Apr. 18th		Firing and weather as on previous day.	
	Apr. 19th		Firing and weather as on previous day.	
	Apr. 20th		Firing as on previous day. Weather showery.	
	Apr. 21st.		Firing and weather as on previous day. The 12 men, attached to the company for a course of instruction in machine gunnery on 31st. March, completed their course and were attached to sections as under:—	
			3 men from 11th Border Regt. attached to No. 1. Section.	
			3 " " 2nd K.O.Y.L.I. " " No. 2. "	
			3 " " 16th. H.L.I. " " No. 3. "	
			3 " " 17th. H.L.I. " " No. 4 "	
			These men took their places in the trenches with their respective sections.	
	Apr. 22nd		At 9.30 p.m. the 17th Battn. H.L.I. made a raid on the enemy's trenches in the THIEPVAL sector; in this operation they were	

T2131. Wt. W708—776. 500000. 4/15. Sir J. C. & S.

Instructions regarding War Diaries and Intelligence Summaries are contained in F. S. Regs., Part II. and the Staff Manual respectively. Title pages will be prepared in manuscript.

~~WAR DIARY~~
or
INTELLIGENCE SUMMARY.
(Erase heading not required.)

Place	Date 1916	Hour	Summary of Events and Information	Remarks and references to Appendices
BOUZINCOURT	Apr. 22nd		assisted by the artillery and 97th M. G. Coy. Two of the machine guns in AUTHUILE WOOD under 2nd Lt. ELLISTON fired at THIEPVAL VILLAGE (Ref. map, FRANCE, sheet 57D, S.E., edition 2, square R 25). Three guns under 2nd Lt. CRAVEN fired at the same place, as well as the reserve gun, which had been brought up from BOUZINCOURT, under 2nd Lt. JINKS and placed in THIEPVAL WOOD. The gun at BRIDGE HEAD fired as usual (see Apr. 13th). The scheme of operations was that the artillery and machine guns should open an intense bombardment at 9.30 pm and continue for 19½ minutes, when they should cease fire for half a minute; by this time the raiding party would be back in our own trenches. The artillery and machine guns were then to bombard for another 30 minutes in order to prevent a counter-attack. Fortunately the raid was a success, the raiding party bringing back 13 prisoners. Our guns fired well, but more belt-filling machines should have been used for such a prolonged bombardment.	

T2134. Wt. W708–776. 500000. 4/15. Sir J. C. & S.

Army Form C. 2118.

Instructions regarding War Diaries and Intelligence Summaries are contained in F. S. Regs., Part II. and the Staff Manual respectively. Title pages will be prepared in manuscript.

WAR DIARY
or
~~INTELLIGENCE SUMMARY.~~
(*Erase heading not required.*)

Place	Date 1916	Hour	Summary of Events and Information	Remarks and references to Appendices
BOUZINCOURT	Apr. 23rd		The day was fine, but no firing was done except by one of the guns from the BRIDGE HEAD defences.	
	Apr. 24th		By 2.30 pm. the company was relieved by the 96th MACHINE GUN COMPANY. The headquarters, with sections 3+4, went into billets at WARLOY, occupying the same billets as previously. Sections 1+2, under 2nd LT. ELLISTON, were billeted in AVELUY (Ref. map, France, No 11, LENS, square 6 H) for the defence of the village. The transport belonging to sections 1+2 remained at BOUZINCOURT. The party in AVELUY relieved a party of the 14th MACHINE GUN COMPANY, and was rationed by the 96th MACHINE GUN COMPANY, being under the command of the O.C., 96th MACHINE GUN COMPANY. Weather fine.	
WARLOY	Apr. 25th		2nd Lt. ELLISTON proceeded to WARLOY, leaving 2nd Lt. JINKS in charge of the party at AVELUY. This party provided two working parties of 1 N.C.O. and 12 men each to make, and improve existing, machine gun emplacements in AVELUY under the supervision of the R.E.'s. Sections 3+4 cleaned up guns and limbers.	

T2134. Wt. W708–776. 500000. 4/15. Sir J. C. & S.

Instructions regarding War Diaries and Intelligence Summaries are contained in F. S. Regs., Part II. and the Staff Manual respectively. Title pages will be prepared in manuscript.

or

INTELLIGENCE SUMMARY.

(Erase heading not required.)

Place	Date 1916	Hour	Summary of Events and Information	Remarks and references to Appendices
WARLOY	Apr. 26th		The party at AVELUY continued their work on the machine gun emplacements. The rest of the company paraded for physical drill under 2nd Lt. N.L.S. POWNALL at 9.00 am and afterwards for gun drill by sections. Weather fine.	
	Apr. 27th		The company took part in a field day operation at BAIZIEUZ, at which all the 32nd DIVISION was represented. In accordance with instructions from BRIGADE HEADQUARTERS, No. 3 Section, under 2nd Lt. CRAVEN, with four guns, was attached to the battalion in reserve, 2nd K.O.Y.L.I., while No. 4 Section, under Lt. WALLACE, with 4 guns, was attached to the battalion in support, 17th. H.L.I. The work alloted was to advance with the battalions and to consolidate certain pre-arranged strong points. LT.-GENERAL SIR T.L.N. MORLAND, G.O.C., X CORPS, and MAJ.-GEN. W.H. RYCROFT, G.O.C., 32nd DIVISION, were both present. Weather very hot.	
	[illegible]		The following reinforcements arrived from the M.G. Base:— 14882 L/Cpl. Maddox, E.	

T2134. Wt. W708—776. 500000. 4/15. Sir J. C. & S.

Army Form C. 2118.

Instructions regarding War Diaries and Intelligence Summaries are contained in F. S. Regs., Part II. and the Staff Manual respectively. Title pages will be prepared in manuscript.

WAR DIARY
or
~~INTELLIGENCE SUMMARY.~~
(Erase heading not required.)

Place	Date 1916	Hour	Summary of Events and Information	Remarks and references to Appendices
WARLOY	Apr.	27th	9794 Pte. SIMS, J.	
			10197 " PHILPOT, W.	
			The AVELUY party continued its work as on the previous day.	
	Apr.	28th	The Company attended a divisional demonstration of the GERMAN Flammenwerfer and Tear shells at SENLIS (Ref. Map, FRANCE, sheet 57D, S.E., edition 2, square V 9 b.). The demonstration was both interesting & instructive, and some of the men were experimented upon. Weather very hot.	
			The AVELUY party continued its work as on the previous day.	
	Apr.	29th	Another class of 12 men, consisting of 4 men from each of the following battalions, 2nd. K.O.Y.L.I., 16th H.L.I., 17th H.L.I., commenced a course of instruction in machine gunnery under C.S.M. SAVAGE. Weather continues hot.	
	Apr.	30th	At 3.00 p.m. all available officers and N.C.O's. attended a lecture at SENLIS on the "Tactical handling of machine guns." This was given to all units in the 32nd. DIVISION, & MAJ.-GEN. W. R. RYCROFT,	

T2134. Wt. W708—776. 500000. 4/15. Sir J. C. & S.

Army Form C. 2118.

Instructions regarding War Diaries and Intelligence Summaries are contained in F. S. Regs., Part II. and the Staff Manual respectively. Title pages will be prepared in manuscript.

WAR DIARY
or
~~INTELLIGENCE~~ SUMMARY.
(Erase heading not required.)

Place	Date 1916	Hour	Summary of Events and Information	Remarks and references to Appendices
WARLOY	Apr. 30th		G.O.C., 32nd DIVISION, was present. The party at AVELUY, consisting of Sections 1 + 2 was relieved by Sections 3 + 4 under LIEUT. WALLACE.	
			Eric S Elliston, 2nd Lt.	
			W A Stanley Capt. OC 97th Bde M G Coy.	

T2134. Wt. W708—776. 500000. 4/15. Sir J. C. & S.

97th Brigade.
32nd Division.

97th BRIGADE MACHINE GUN COMPANY

M A Y 1 9 1 6

97 M G Coy
Vol. 3

XXXII

Confidential

War Diary of

97th. Brigade Machine Gun Company

from 1st May 1916 to 31st May 1916.

W. W. Stanley CAPTAIN,
O.C. 97 M.G. COY.

Army Form C. 2118.

Instructions regarding War Diaries and Intelligence Summaries are contained in F. S. Regs., Part II. and the Staff Manual respectively. Title pages will be prepared in manuscript.

WAR DIARY
or
~~INTELLIGENCE SUMMARY.~~
(Erase heading not required.)

Place	Date 1916	Hour	Summary of Events and Information	Remarks and references to Appendices
WARLOY	May 1st.		The Company participated in some Field Day Exercises at BAIZIEUZ, similar to those which took place on 27th. ult. MAJ.-GEN. W. R. RYCROFT, G.O.C., 32nd DIVISION, was present. Weather fine & hot.	
	May 2nd.		The Company paraded for Physical Drill under 2nd Lt. N.L.S. POWNALL and cleaning of guns and limbers under section officers. In the afternoon all available officers & men fired a musketry or revolver practise. Weather hot & showery.	
	May 3rd.		The Company took part in a Brigade Tactical Exercise at BAIZIEUZ, similar to that of 1st. inst. Weather a little cooler.	
	May 4th.		The Company took part in a Divisional Tactical Exercise at BAIZIEUZ, similar to that of 1st. inst. MAJ.-GEN. W. R. RYCROFT, G.O.C., 32nd DIVISION, was present. Weather hot. GEN. SIR H. S. RAWLINSON, G.O.C., Fourth Army was also present. LIEUT. C. S. SMITH rejoined the company from the Machine Gun Base.	
	May 5th.		The Company moved to CONTAY (Ref. Map, FRANCE, LENS, 11,	

T2134. Wt. W708–776. 500000. 4/15. Sir J. C. & S.

Instructions regarding War Diaries and Intelligence Summaries are contained in F. S. Regs., Part II. and the Staff Manual respectively. Title pages will be prepared in manuscript.

WAR DIARY
or
~~INTELLIGENCE SUMMARY.~~
(Erase heading not required.)

Army Form C. 2118.

Place	Date 1916	Hour	Summary of Events and Information	Remarks and references to Appendices
WARLOY	May 5th		square F6) taking over billets occupied by the 14th BRIGADE MACHINE GUN COMPANY. The billets were found to be very poor, many of the men preferring to bivouac in an orchard near the limbers. Sections 3 + 4 from AVELUY moved to CONTAY as soon as relieved by the same unit. CORPORAL PARKER commenced a course of Instruction at the DIVISIONAL ANTI-GAS SCHOOL, SENLIS, lasting four days.	
CONTAY	May 6th		The day was largely occupied with fatigues, several working parties being required by the TOWN MAJOR. PTE. W. PHILPOTT reported to the O.C., No. 4 COMPANY, 32nd DIVISIONAL TRAIN, A.S.C., VADENCOURT, (Ref. Map FRANCE, LENS, 11, square F6) for a course of instruction in Saddlery, with a view to becoming the company saddler.	
	May 7th		There was a rifle inspection at 10·30 am. Weather fine + warm.	
	May 8th		All available men of Nos. 3 + 4 Sections fired a musketry or revolver practise. The remainder of the company was fully	

Instructions regarding War Diaries and Intelligence Summaries are contained in F. S. Regs., Part II. and the Staff Manual respectively. Title pages will be prepared in manuscript.

WAR DIARY

or

~~INTELLIGENCE SUMMARY.~~

(Erase heading not required.)

Army Form C. 2118.

Place	Date 1916	Hour	Summary of Events and Information	Remarks and references to Appendices
CONTAY	May 8th		occupied with cleaning up billets, most of which were in a most insanitary condition.	
	May 9th		The company took part in a DIVISIONAL Tactical Excercise similar to that held on 4th inst. LT.-GEN. SIR J.T.N. MORLAND, G.O.C., Xth CORPS, was present. Rainy weather.	
	May 10th		The company paraded under section officers for musketry, gun cleaning, &c. Weather fine.	
	May 11th		The company took part in a BRIGADE Tactical Excercise, similar to that of 9th inst. BRIG-GEN. J.B. JARDINE, G.O.C. 97th BRIGADE was present. One man from each of the four sections commenced a short signalling course under the company signallers with a view to replacing them if necessary. Weather showery	
	May 12th		The company took part in a DIVISIONAL Tactical Excercise, similar to that of 9th. inst. LT.-GEN. SIR T.L.N. MORLAND, G.O.C., Xth ARMY CORPS, was present. Weather fine.	

Army Form C. 2118.

Instructions regarding War Diaries and Intelligence Summaries are contained in F. S. Regs., Part II. and the Staff Manual respectively. Title pages will be prepared in manuscript.

WAR DIARY
or
~~INTELLIGENCE SUMMARY.~~

(Erase heading not required.)

Place	Date 1916	Hour	Summary of Events and Information	Remarks and references to Appendices
CONTAY	May 13th		CORPORAL PARKER, who had attended a DIVISIONAL Gas Course, commenced giving lectures on the subject to each section; the lectures were accompanied with helmet drill. Three officers attended a lecture on "The Battle of LOOS" given at SENLIS by Lt.-COL. WACE. Weather wet in morning, but fine in afternoon.	
	May 14th		The water-cart was sent to WARLOY to be repaired at the ORDNANCE WORKSHOPS there. The company was to have bivouaced out for the night with the rest of the brigade, but the operations were cancelled on account of the wet weather and consequent damage to crops. Baths were arranged for the men. Weather changeable & cold.	
	May 15th		The morning was spent on fatigues, and the company went for a short route march in the afternoon. Weather changeable.	
	May 16th		The day was well spent in clearing up & cleaning up guns, &c. and repacking the limbers, prior to going into the line again.	

Army Form C. 2118.

Instructions regarding War Diaries and Intelligence Summaries are contained in F. S. Regs., Part II. and the Staff Manual respectively. Title pages will be prepared in manuscript.

WAR DIARY
or
~~INTELLIGENCE~~ SUMMARY.
(Erase heading not required.)

Place	Date 1916	Hour	Summary of Events and Information	Remarks and references to Appendices
CONTAY	May 17th		Sections 1 + 3 under LIEUT. SMITH proceeded to AVELUY taking over the defences of that place from the 96th BRIGADE MACHINE GUN CO. The remainder of the company under CAPT. STANLEY proceeded to WARLOY, exchanging billets with the 96th BRIGADE MACHINE GUN CO. In the afternoon CAPT. STANLEY, LIEUT. WALLACE, 2nd LIEUT. LAVENDER and 2nd LIEUT. POWNALL attended a lecture at SENLIS by LIEUT.-COL. WACE on "The Tactical Handling of Machine Guns". Weather very hot.	
WARLOY	May 18th		The company took up its position in the line, relieving the 14th BRIGADE MACHINE GUN COMPANY. The relief was complete by 3·30 p.m. CAPT. STANLEY, LIEUT. SMITH and the headquarters of the company proceeded to its old quarters at BOUZINCOURT (Ref. Map, FRANCE, 57D, SE, square W7). Fifteen guns took up positions as shewn on the accompanying map, (Appendix I) each position being marked with numbers 1 – 15. The sixteenth gun was kept in reserve at Headquarters at BOUZINCOURT for instructional purposes. The relief was somewhat delayed owing to an active bombardment	

T2134. Wt. W708—776. 500000. 4/15. Sir J. C. & S.

Instructions regarding War Diaries and Intelligence Summaries are contained in F. S. Regs., Part II. and the Staff Manual respectively. Title pages will be prepared in manuscript.

WAR DIARY
or
~~INTELLIGENCE~~ SUMMARY.
(Erase heading not required.)

Army Form C. 2118.

Place	Date 1916	Hour	Summary of Events and Information	Remarks and references to Appendices
WARLOY	May	18th	by the enemy. The parties relieved by us seemed very glad to be relieved, reporting that the enemy was very vigorous during their spell in the trenches. They seemed more nervous than the position warranted. During the night Nos. 14 + 15 guns at BRIDGE HEAD fired intermittently over AUTHUILE WOOD at the trenches in and around THIEPVAL VILLAGE. Weather very hot.	
BOUZINCOURT	May	19th	The company sustained its second casualty in the morning, No. 8479 Pte. OWEN, H. J., being wounded in the neck by a machine gun bullet at point W.6.a.36 (Ref. map, FRANCE, sheet 57D, SE, edition 2). Between 9.00 + 10.00 pm. No. 5 gun fired traversing along the road marked THIEPVAL ROAD in square R.25 (Ref. map, FRANCE, sheet 57D, S.E edition 2). Nos. 14 + 15 guns fired at enemy's trenches round OVILLERS in squares X 2, 8 + 14 (same reference), intermittently during the night.	
	May	20th	No. 5 gun was moved from COCKEYMORE STREET to an emplacement in THIEPVAL AVENUE marked 5a on accompanying map (appendix I). During the night Nos. 6, 7, 3 + 4 guns fired intermittently on and around THIEPVAL VILLAGE	

Army Form C. 2118.

WAR DIARY
or
~~INTELLIGENCE SUMMARY.~~
(Erase heading not required.)

Instructions regarding War Diaries and Intelligence Summaries are contained in F. S. Regs., Part II. and the Staff Manual respectively. Title pages will be prepared in manuscript.

Place	Date 1916	Hour	Summary of Events and Information	Remarks and references to Appendices
BOUZINCOURT	May 20th.		Nos. 14 + 15 guns fired as on the preceding night. Weather continues hot.	
	May 21st.		No. 8479, Pte. OWEN, H.J., wounded, was evacuated to C.C.S. A lot of work was done in improving the gun position No. 9, which was taken over in a very battered about condition; a scheme was made up to sandbag all the approaches to it. Between 8.50 pm. + 9.30 pm. No. 7 gun fired at the cross roads in square R32a, same reference, as enemy transport had been heard in that direction on the two preceding evenings. Between 9.30 pm and midnight No. 6 gun fired at the enemy barbed wire in front of his trenches in squares X1a and X1b, this having been cut by our artillery at 6.30 pm. At the same time Nos. 3 + 4 and 14 guns fired at the ~~OVILLERS~~ POZIERES - THIEPVAL road in square R26c, same reference, information being received from the infantry that enemy transport was heard in abundance in that direction. Weather very hot.	
	May 22nd		Five of the men undergoing the course of instruction under S-M. SAVAGE went up to the trenches for instruction. A party of 3 N.C.O's and 11 men were returned to the base as being unsuitable for machine gun work.	

T2134. Wt. W708—776. 500000. 4/15. Sir J. C. & S.

Instructions regarding War Diaries and Intelligence Summaries are contained in F. S. Regs., Part II. and the Staff Manual respectively. Title pages will be prepared in manuscript.

WAR DIARY
or
~~INTELLIGENCE SUMMARY.~~
(Erase heading not required.)

Army Form C. 2118.

Place	Date 1916	Hour	Summary of Events and Information	Remarks and references to Appendices
BOUZINCOURT	May	22nd.	Nos. 6 + 7 guns fired as on the previous day. Nos. 14 + 15 guns fired during the night traversing the enemy trenches between OVILLERS and THIEPVAL VILLAGES.	
	May	23rd.	A reinforcement of 8 men arrived from the Base; four of these seem fairly smart but four certainly will need further instruction and are therefore attached to the class under S-M. SAVAGE. The following beasts were also drawn for the company:- two light draught horses for G.S. wagon; one rider for the transport sergeant; two mules, to replace two sick ones. The mules are good animals, but the horses are a poor class. Nos. 6 + 7, and 14 and 15 guns fired as on the previous day. It rained all the afternoon making the trenches very very muddy.	
	May	24th	A portion of the parapet next to CHECQUERBENT ST. was blown in by enemy artillery and was repaired at night. Nos. 14 + 15 guns fired as on the previous day. Also Nos. 3 + 4 as on 21st. inst. There was rain all day.	
	May	25th	Nos. 7911, Pte. LONG, W. and No. 7932, Pte BLYTHE, R. were evacuated to C.C.S., both being sick. Nos. 14 + 15 guns fired as usual, and 3 + 4 as on previous day. The weather was dull all day with occasional showers of rain.	

Instructions regarding War Diaries and Intelligence Summaries are contained in F. S. Regs., Part II. and the Staff Manual respectively. Title pages will be prepared in manuscript.

Army Form C. 2118.

WAR DIARY
or
~~INTELLIGENCE SUMMARY.~~
(Erase heading not required.)

Place	Date 1916	Hour	Summary of Events and Information	Remarks and references to Appendices
BOUZINCOURT	May	26th	At 3.15 pm. an enemy H.E. shell burst on the No. 9 gun dug-out wrecking it completely. Fortunately it was not being used except as an ammunition store, all of which was recovered; a few spare parts were buried. At night the parapet was fairly well repaired. Nos. 3, 4, 6, 7, 14 + 15 guns fired as usual. All guns near the front line "stood to" all night on account of an expected raid.	
	May	27th	No. 3 gun was moved to a fresh position marked 3a on accompanying map, (Appendix I). No. 1 gun fired a few rounds at 9.45 pm. at the enemy barbed wire exactly opposite as an enemy working party was reported there. The Nos 3, 4, 6, 7, 14 + 15 guns fired as usual. The weather was finer.	
	May	28th	A rocket test was carried out by the 11th. BORDER REGIMENT soon after 9.00 pm. It was only partially successful as the rockets could not be seen from several of our guns positions. The enemy opened fire as soon as the rockets went up, but did not continue for long. Nos. 6 + 7 guns fired as usual. The day was fairly quiet, and also the night. Weather fine.	
	May	29th	A small patrol of 1 officer and 2 men went out in front of gun position 9	

T2134. Wt. W708—776. 500000. 4/15. Sir J. C. & S.

Instructions regarding War Diaries and Intelligence Summaries are contained in F. S. Regs., Part II. and the Staff Manual respectively. Title pages will be prepared in manuscript.

WAR DIARY
or
~~INTELLIGENCE SUMMARY.~~
(Erase heading not required.)

Army Form C. 2118.

Place	Date 1916	Hour	Summary of Events and Information	Remarks and references to Appendices
OUZINCOURT	May 29th		to inspect our barbed wire there; it returned safely at 10·30 p.m. after being out for 20 minutes. During the day the parados near gun position 10 was blown in by an H.E. shell and was repaired at night. Nos. 6, 7, 14 + 15 guns fired as usual during the night. It rained all the afternoon + evening.	
	May 30th		The company was relieved in the line by the 96th BRIGADE MACHINE GUN COMPANY, the relief being completed by 4·00 p.m. Sections 1 + 2 proceeded to AVELUY, under 2nd LT. JINKS, for the defence of that place, while HEADQUARTERS and Sections 3 + 4 proceeded to WARLOY to the same billets there as before. Weather fine.	
	May 31st		The day was spent in cleaning up guns + equipment. A kit inspection was also held at 2·00 p.m. Baths were provided for the men during the morning. The weather was fine + warm.	

W A Stanley CAPTAIN,
O.C. 97 M.G. COY.

Eric S. Elliston 2/Lt.

T2134. Wt. W708–776. 500000. 4/15. Sir J. C. & S.

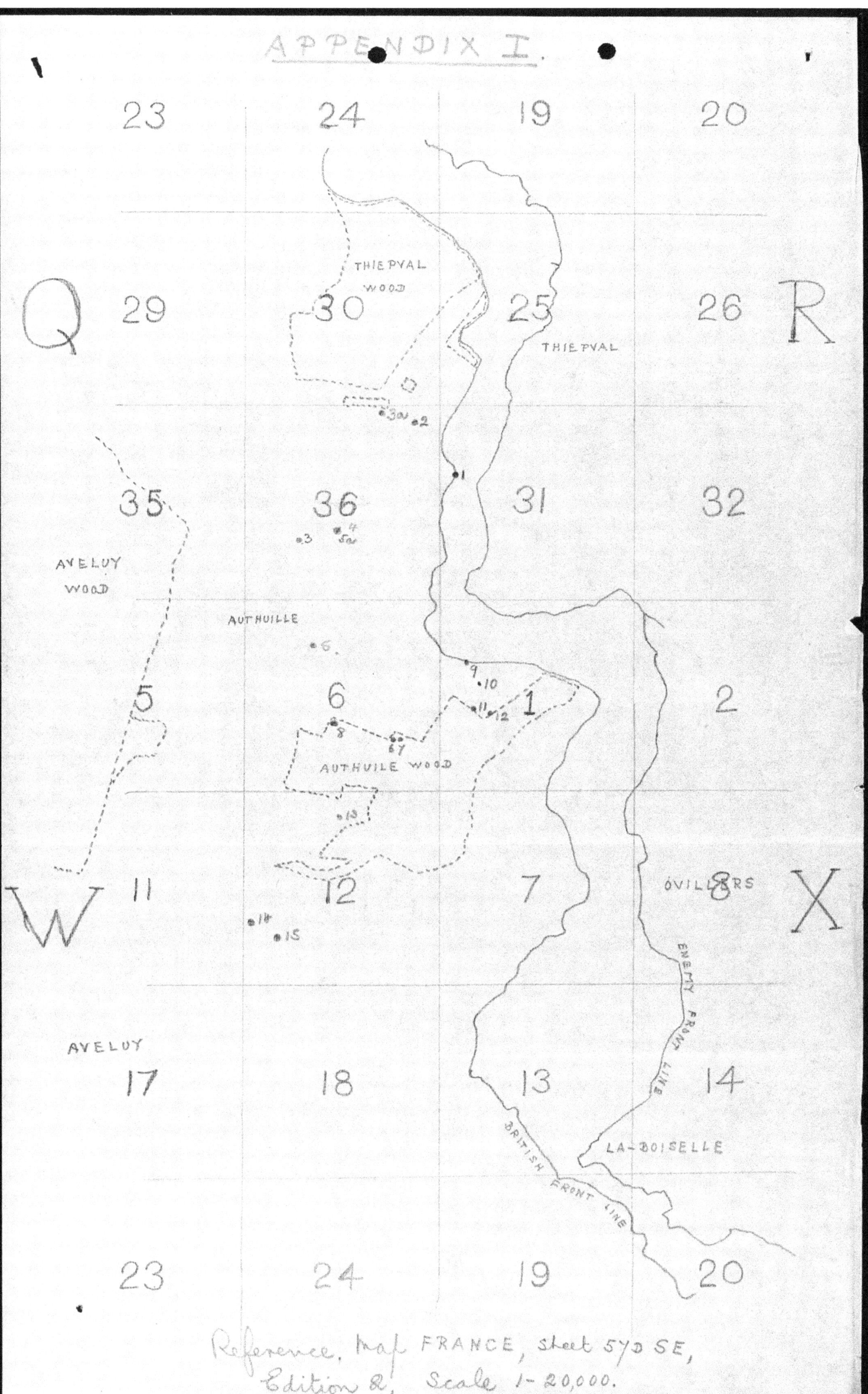
APPENDIX I. 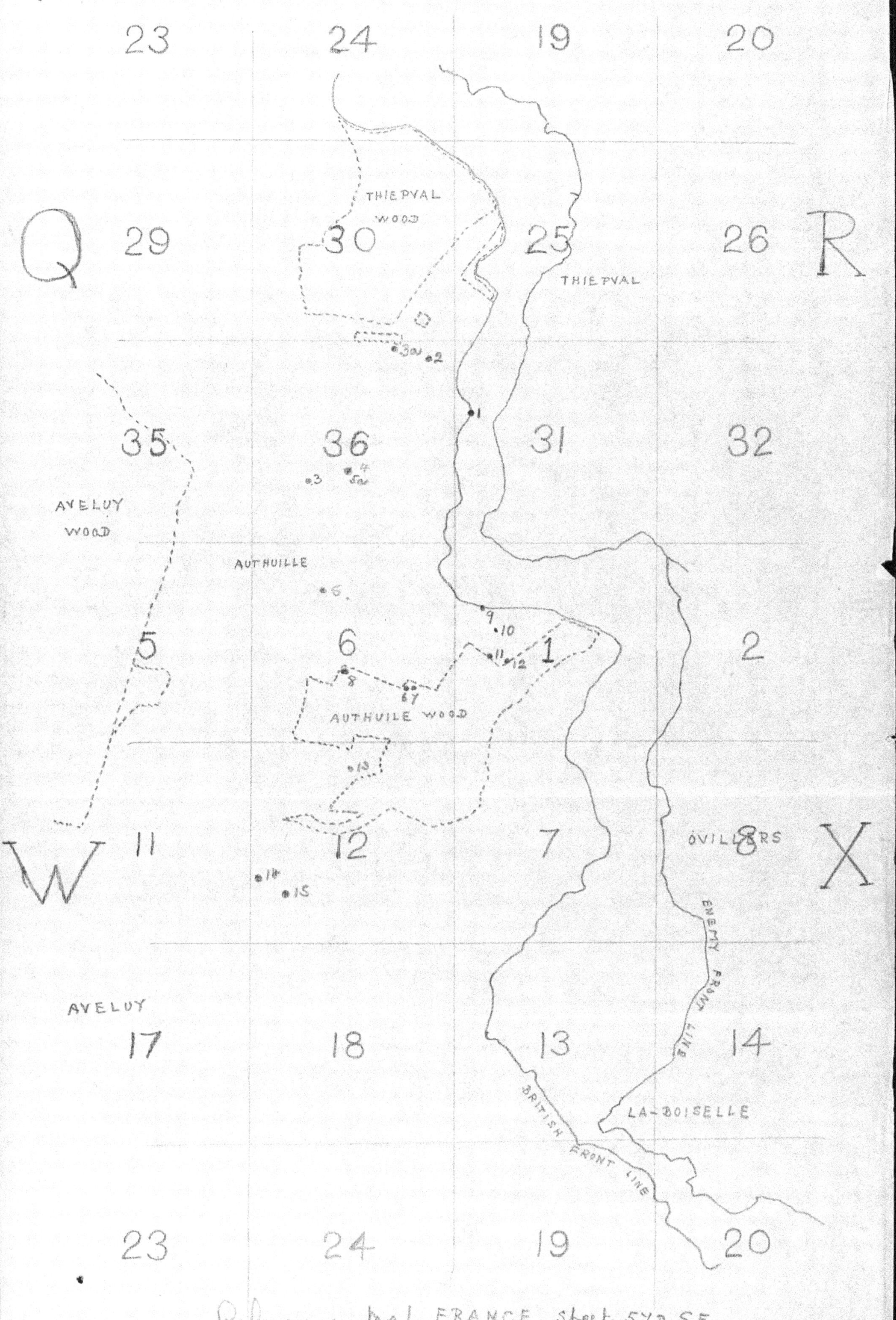
Q
R
W
X
THIEPVAL WOOD
THIEPVAL
AVELUY WOOD
AUTHUILLE
AUTHUILE WOOD
OVILLERS
ENEMY FRONT LINE
BRITISH FRONT LINE
LA-BOISELLE
AVELUY
Reference, Map FRANCE, Sheet 57D SE,
Edition 2, Scale 1-20,000.

97th Brigade.

32nd Division.

97th BRIGADE MACHINE GUN COMPANY

J U N E 1 9 1 6

Confidential

97. MGC

War Diary of

Vol 4

97th. Brigade Machine Gun Coy.

from 1st. June 1916 to 30th June 1916.

W A Stanley Capt Commanding,
97th BDE. MACHINE GUN COY.

Instructions regarding War Diaries and Intelligence Summaries are contained in F. S. Regs., Part II. and the Staff Manual respectively. Title pages will be prepared in manuscript.

XXXII

WAR DIARY
or
~~INTELLIGENCE~~ SUMMARY.
(Erase heading not required.)

Army Form C. 2118.

Place	Date	Hour	Summary of Events and Information	Remarks and references to Appendices
	1916			
WARLOY	June	1st.	The Company at WARLOY took part in Divisional Tactical Exercises similar to those held on 12th. May. MAJ.-GEN. W. R. RYCROFT, G. O. C., 32nd DIVISION was present. The party at AVELUY, consisting of Nos 1 + 2 Sections supplied working parties to construct machine gun emplacements in the trenches. An enemy shell burst among one of these working parties unfortunately causing the following casualties:-	Map of FRANCE Sheet 57D 1:40,000 square W.14.
			No. 8466, Pte. PHILLIPS, L. severely wounded.	
			No. 7904, Pte. MILLER, G. slightly wounded.	
			No. 7894, Pte. CAMPBELL, W. slightly wounded.	
			No. 7897, Pte. WOODHOUSE, C. slightly wounded.	
			Of these, PTE. PHILLIPS, L. died in hospital at 8.45 p.m.; PTE. MILLER, G. was admitted to hospital, while the other two were well enough to return to their section. Weather fine + warm.	
	June	2nd.	Sections 3 + 4 at WARLOY paraded for drill under section officers. The AVELUY party provided trench working parties as before. PTE. PHILLIPS, L.	Ref. as above square U.24

T2134. Wt. W708–776. 500000. 4/15. Sir J. C. & S.

Army Form C. 2118.

Instructions regarding War Diaries and Intelligence Summaries are contained in F. S. Regs., Part II. and the Staff Manual respectively. Title pages will be prepared in manuscript.

WAR DIARY
or
~~INTELLIGENCE SUMMARY~~.
(Erase heading not required.)

Place	Date 1916	Hour	Summary of Events and Information	Remarks and references to Appendices
WARLOY	June	2nd	was buried at WARLOY CEMETERY, CAPT. W. A. STANLEY, 2nd LIEUT. E. S. ELLISTON, a sergeant and 12 men attending the funeral. A sum of Fifty Francs was alloted to the company as our share of the profits of the Divisional Canteens; this sum was handed over to 2nd LIEUT. N. L. S. POWNALL to go towards the company SPORTS FUND. No 7904, Pte. MILLER G. was evacuated to the C.C.S. Weather fine & hot.	
	June	3rd.	The AVELUY party supplied working parties for the trenches. During the afternoon No. 15143 Pte. CUMMING, A., attached from the 16th Bn. H.L.I. was slightly wounded, but not seriously enough to be admitted to hospital. The men at WARLOY paraded under section officers in the morning & had a holiday in the afternoon. Weather fine.	
	June	4th.	Nos. 1 & 2 Sections at AVELUY proceeded to WARLOY upon being relieved by Nos. 3 & 4 Sections under 2nd LIEUTS. CRAVEN and POWNALL. A further 12 men, being three men from each of the four infantry battalions in the brigade, commenced a course of instruction on machine guns under C.S.M. SAVAGE.	

T2134. Wt. W708—776. 500000. 4/15. Sir J. C. & S.

Instructions regarding War Diaries and Intelligence Summaries are contained in F. S. Regs., Part II. and the Staff Manual respectively. Title pages will be prepared in manuscript.

WAR DIARY
or
~~INTELLIGENCE~~ SUMMARY.

(*Erase heading not required.*)

Army Form C. 2118.

Place	Date 1916	Hour	Summary of Events and Information	Remarks and references to Appendices
WARLOY	June	5th	Working parties were supplied by the party at AVELUY. The remainder paraded at WARLOY under section officers. Weather showery.	
	June	6th	Working parties were supplied by the party at AVELUY. The remainder paraded at WARLOY under section officers. Weather showery.	
	June	7th	Same as 6th inst.	
	June	8th	Working parties were supplied by the party at AVELUY. The remainder took part in a Divisional Tactical Excercise similar to that of 1st. inst. MAJ.-GEN. W. R. RYCROFT, G. O. C., 32nd DIVISION, was present. Weather fine.	
	June	9th	Same as 7th. inst. 2nd LT. T. W. GREGG reported his arrival from the MACHINE GUN BASE and is attached to No. 1. Section. Weather showery.	
	June	10th	Same as 9th. inst. Weather wet. No. 7882, Pte. LUND, E returned from a Shoeing Course at the DIVISIONAL FORGE. Capt. W. A. STANLEY	
	~~June~~	~~11th~~	went home on leave, LIEUT. C. S. SMITH assuming command of the company.	
	June	11th	Same as 10th. inst. Weather showery. 2nd LIEUTS. LAVENDER and HANNAH attended a lecture at SENLIS by MAJOR WALLACE on	Ref. map. as above square V 16 d 7

T2134. Wt. W708–776. 500000. 4/15. Sir J. C. & S.

Army Form C. 2118.

Instructions regarding War Diaries and Intelligence Summaries are contained in F. S. Regs., Part II. and the Staff Manual respectively. Title pages will be prepared in manuscript.

WAR DIARY
or
~~INTELLIGENCE SUMMARY.~~
(Erase heading not required.)

Place	Date 1916	Hour	Summary of Events and Information	Remarks and references to Appendices
WARLOY	June	11th	his experiences in the recent naval battle off JUTLAND.	
	June	12th	The part of the company at WARLOY took part in a DIVISIONAL Tactical Excercise similar to that of 8th. inst. When the excercise was over the company proceeded to CONTAY taking over billets vacated by the 14th. BRIGADE MACHINE GUN COMPANY. There was a slight improvement in the billets alloted to us, part of them having been bunked with wire beds. Billets vacated by us at WARLOY were handed over to the 14th. BRIGADE MACHINE GUN COMPANY. The party at AVELUY, on being relieved by a party of the 14th BRIGADE MACHINE GUN COMPANY, joined the company at CONTAY. Rain in morning, but finer later on.	Ref. Map as above square U 27 + 26
CONTAY	June	13th	The company paraded for excercise under section officers. No. 11290, Pte. MIDDLETON, who was wounded slightly in the thigh on 11th. inst. was evacuated to the C.C.S. No. 7925, Cpl. CHAPRELLE was evacuated to the C.C.S. with German measles. There was a full Company parade at 5.30 p.m. reorganising the various	

T2134. Wt. W708—776. 500000. 4/15. Sir J. C. & S.

Instructions regarding War Diaries and Intelligence Summaries are contained in F. S. Regs., Part II. and the Staff Manual respectively. Title pages will be prepared in manuscript.

WAR DIARY
or
~~INTELLIGENCE SUMMARY~~.
(Erase heading not required.)

Army Form C. 2118.

Place	Date 1916	Hour	Summary of Events and Information	Remarks and references to Appendices
CONTAY	June 13th.		sections, some of which had become rather weak by casualties, transfers, &c. Weather fine.	
	June 14th.		The Company paraded under section officers. Great attention was paid to having the whole company absolutely prepared to take part in any advance which might take place. No. 7881, Pte. DOHERTY, P. proceeded to SENLIS to attend a course of shoeing at the DIVISIONAL FORGE. All watches were put on one hour at midnight in accordance with arrangements made by the French Government.	
	June 15th.		The Company took part in a Tactical Exercise similar to that on 12th. inst. LIEUT.-GEN. SIR T. L. N. MORLAND, G.O.C., X Corps, was present.	
	June 16th.		The Company paraded under section officers. Each section in turn proceeded to the trenches near WARLOY to practise making emplacements rapidly. Weather fine.	Ref. Map as above Point V23a 05
	June 17th.		Same as 16th. inst. No. 10197, Pte PHILPOT, W. returned from a	

T2134. Wt. W708—776. 500000. 4/15. Sir J. C. & S.

Instructions regarding War Diaries and Intelligence Summaries are contained in F. S. Regs., Part II. and the Staff Manual respectively. Title pages will be prepared in manuscript.

WAR DIARY
or
~~INTELLIGENCE SUMMARY.~~
(Erase heading not required.)

Army Form C. 2118.

Place	Date 1916	Hour	Summary of Events and Information	Remarks and references to Appendices
CONTAY	June	17th	course in Saddlery with the A.S.C. and is appointed Company Saddler.	
	June	18th	The Company attended a Brigade Church Parade on the Sports Ground at 10.45 a.m. at which MAJ.-GEN. W. R. RYCROFT, G.O.C., 32nd. DIV. was present. Weather fine.	
	June	19th	The Company took part in a Brigade Tactical Exercise similar to that of 15th. inst. Capt. W. A. STANLEY reassumed command of the Company on returning from leave. Weather showery.	
	June	20th	The Company took part in a Divisional Tactical Exercise similar to that of 19th. inst. Immediately after the exercise, the company, acting under orders from the Brigade, proceeded to point V23.a.22 to attend a Gas Demonstration. On arrival at the place no sign whatever was visible of the demonstration, so the company returned to billets in CONTAY, when it was found out that the Brigade had ordered us to point <u>V</u>23.a.22 instead of <u>U</u>23.a.22. Weather fine.	Ref. Map as above.

Instructions regarding War Diaries and Intelligence Summaries are contained in F. S. Regs., Part II. and the Staff Manual respectively. Title pages will be prepared in manuscript.

WAR DIARY
or
~~INTELLIGENCE~~ SUMMARY.
(Erase heading not required.)

Army Form C. 2118.

Place	Date 1916	Hour	Summary of Events and Information	Remarks and references to Appendices
CONTAY	June	21st	The Company attended a Gas Demonstration by LIEUT. SHARRATT at point U23.a.22 at 10.00 am. No. 31712, Pte. DEEGAN, G. reported his arrival from the base as spare transport driver.	
	June	22nd	The Company vacated billets at CONTAY and proceeded to BOUZINCOURT, arriving there at 11.30 pm. This day was known as "S" day. Weather fine. Company stores were left at CONTAY in charge of the TOWN MAJOR, the company leaving one man as guard.	Ref. Map as above square W.7.
BOUZINCOURT	June	23rd	The Company proceeded at separate times in the afternoon to pre-arranged points in the trenches, relieving the 14th. BRIGADE MACHINE GUN COMPANY. No. 1 Section proceeded to BRIDGE HEAD DEFENCES; No. 2 Section to dugouts at CRUCIFIX CORNER; No. 3 Section to AUTHUILLE DEFENCES; and No. 4 Section to emplacements in AUTHUILE WOOD known as LOMOND POST and DUMBARTON CASTLE. COMPANY HEADQUARTERS were at the BRIGADE BATTLE POSITION near AUTHUILLE WOOD. 2nd LIEUT. CRAVEN and one gun team from each of Nos. 3 + 4 Sections remained as reserve at BOUZINCOURT; the transport and Quartermaster Stores also	square X.18a square X.18a square W.6a square W.6d. square W.12a

T2134. Wt. W708—776. 500000. 4/15. Sir J. C. & S.

Instructions regarding War Diaries and Intelligence Summaries are contained in F. S. Regs., Part II. and the Staff Manual respectively. Title pages will be prepared in manuscript.

WAR DIARY
or
~~INTELLIGENCE~~ SUMMARY.
(Erase heading not required.)

Army Form C. 2118.

Place	Date 1916	Hour	Summary of Events and Information	Remarks and references to Appendices
BOUZINCOURT	June	23rd	remained at BOUZINCOURT. Weather showery. This day was known as "T" day. During the night Nos. 3 + 4 Sections guns fired at the enemy front line trenches and wire in squares R 25 and 31. Two guns belonging to No. 1 Section also fired at the same points. The company transport was taken charge of by the BRIGADE TRANSPORT OFFICER.	Ref. map as above
AUTHUILLE	June	24th	There was increased artillery activity along the whole front. One gun and team took up its position at the VALLEY EMPLACEMENT at point W 12.b.08. This gun belonged to No. 1 Section. Guns at BRIDGE HEAD DEFENCES and AUTHUILLE fired during the night intermittently as on 23rd. inst. Weather showery. This day was known as "U" day.	
	June	25th	The day passed much the same as 24th inst., during the evening the enemy sending over a number of tear shells. During the night one gun belonging to No. 2 Section and one gun of No. 4 Section were mounted at CONISTON POST and fired at enemy trenches in R 32 a.	square X.7 a

Instructions regarding War Diaries and Intelligence Summaries are contained in F. S. Regs., Part II. and the Staff Manual respectively. Title pages will be prepared in manuscript.

WAR DIARY

or

~~INTELLIGENCE~~ SUMMARY.

(Erase heading not required.)

Army Form C. 2118.

Place	Date 1916	Hour	Summary of Events and Information	Remarks and references to Appendices
AUTHUILLE	June 25th		During the day, exact time unknown, No. 14570, Pte OWENS, G. was killed by shrapnel near AUTHUILLE WOOD. Weather fine: This day was known as "V" day.	
	June 26th		The day passed very much the same as 25th. inst.; the enemy bombarded AUTHUILLE WOOD very heavily. The guns at BRIDGE HEAD and one gun at CONISTON POST fired intermittently during the night at same points as before. Weather very showery. This day was known as "W" day.	
	June 27th.		Artillery activity as before. Two guns at BRIDGE HEAD and one at CONISTON POST fired as on previous night. Thorough preparations were made during these few last days for the proposed general advance on "Z" day, DUMBARTON CASTLE being prepared as the Company headquarters and store. A lot of rain fell during the day, the wind remaining north and north-easterly. This day was known as X day.	
	June 28th		At 3.00 p.m. all packs + surplus kits were dumped at CRUCIFIX CORNER	

Instructions regarding War Diaries and Intelligence Summaries are contained in F. S. Regs., Part II. and the Staff Manual respectively. Title pages will be prepared in manuscript.

WAR DIARY

or

~~INTELLIGENCE SUMMARY.~~

(Erase heading not required.)

Army Form C. 2118.

Place	Date 1916	Hour	Summary of Events and Information	Remarks and references to Appendices
AUTHUILLE	June 28th		and later in the day removed by our limbers and stocked at BOUZINCOURT. All sections were ready to take up their battle positions, as prearranged, but these movements were cancelled early in the afternoon owing to the postponement of Z day. During the night two guns of No. 4 Section at CONISTON POST and two at BRIDGE HEAD fired intermittently at same points as before. Considerable rain fell during the morning, but the evening was fine. This day was known as "Y" day.	
	June 29th		The artillery was active as on the preceding days on both sides. During the night two guns of No. 2 Section from CONISTON POST and two guns of No. 1. Section from BRIDGE HEAD fired intermittently at same points as before. Weather was finer, with wind in same direction. Near AUTHUILLE VILLAGE, No. 3622, Pte. TAYLOR, S, 16th. H.L.I attached, was slightly wounded in the arm by shrapnel, but not badly enough to be sent back. This day was known as Y1 day.	

T2134. Wt. W708—776. 500000. 4/15. Sir J. C. & S.

Instructions regarding War Diaries and Intelligence Summaries are contained in F. S. Regs., Part II. and the Staff Manual respectively. Title pages will be prepared in manuscript.

WAR DIARY
or
~~INTELLIGENCE SUMMARY.~~
(Erase heading not required.)

Army Form C. 2118.

Place	Date 1916	Hour	Summary of Events and Information	Remarks and references to Appendices
AUTHUILLE	June	30th	Artillery was again active on both sides. During the evening the various sections took up their battle positions as follows:-	
			No. 1. Section, 2nd LIEUTS. JINKS + GREGG, with four guns at KINTYRE TRENCH.	Ref. Maps as above square W 6. b.
			No. 2. Section, 2nd. LIEUTS. ELLISTON + LAVENDER, with four guns in AUTHUILLE WOOD TRENCHES.	square W 6. d.
			No. 3. Section, 2nd LIEUT. HANNAH, with four guns at DUMBARTON CASTLE.	square W 6. d.
			No. 4. Section, LIEUT. WALLACE + 2nd. LIEUT. POWNALL, with four guns at LOMOND POST.	square W 6. c.
			CAPT. W. A. STANLEY, O.C., COMPANY, had his headquarters with the G.O.C., 97th. Inf. Brigade, near AUTHUILLE WOOD.	square W 12. a.
			LIEUT. C. S. SMITH, in charge of ammunition and stores was at DUMBARTON CASTLE.	
			These movements were completed by 10.00 p.m. The weather was finer on the whole. This day was known as "Y 2" day. Eric S. Elliston 2/Lieut.	

T2134. Wt. W708–776. 500000. 4/15. Sir J. C. & S.

97th Inf.Bde.
32nd Div.

97th MACHINE GUN COMPANY.

J U L Y

1 9 1 6

HEADQUARTERS
No. ....
Date 31.7.16.
97th MACHINE GUN COY

Vol 5

War Diary

of the

97th Machine Gun Company

covering the period.

July 1st 1916 to July 31st 1916

W.A. Stanley Capt.
Commanding,
97 MACHINE GUN COY.

Instructions regarding War Diaries and Intelligence Summaries are contained in F. S. Regs., Part II. and the Staff Manual respectively. Title pages will be prepared in manuscript.

ORIGINAL

WAR DIARY
or
~~INTELLIGENCE~~ SUMMARY.
(Erase heading not required.)

Army Form C. 2118.

Place	Date	Hour	Summary of Events and Information	Remarks and references to Appendices
AUTHUILLE.	1/7/16	7·30am	The four sections of the company were in the battle positions taken up on the previous night as follows:–	
			No. 1. Sectn KINTYRE TRENCH with two Coys of the 2nd K.O.Y.L.I	
			" 2 " AUTHUILLE WOOD trenches with two Coys of the XI Border Regt.	
			" 3 " In brigade reserve at DUMBARTON CASTLE (AUTHUILLE WOOD).	
			" 4 " Two guns in brigade reserve at LOMOND POST (do do)	
			Two guns in CONNISTON HILL TRENCH.	
			Under perfect weather conditions the general attack commenced at 7·30 am after 65 mins. furious Artillery bombardment, and at just after 8 am. No 1 & No 2 Section left their trenches with the KOYLI (on the left) and the Border Regt. (on the right) & from here we will follow the movements of the two sections separately.	
		8·0am	No 1 Sectn 2 guns under 2/Lt JINKS were attached to one KOYLI Coy & reached the German 2nd line and installed themselves in rough emplacements in the parados of this trench by 9·0 am with only one casualty. Owing to a bad field of fire & the ground in front of them being covered by	

T2134. Wt. W708–776. 500000. 4/15. Sir J. C. & S.

Instructions regarding War Diaries and Intelligence Summaries are contained in F. S. Regs., Part II. and the Staff Manual respectively. Title pages will be prepared in manuscript.

WAR DIARY
or
INTELLIGENCE SUMMARY.
(Erase heading not required.)

Army Form C. [illegible]118.

Place	Date	Hour	Summary of Events and Information	Remarks and references to Appendices
AUTHUILLE	1/7/16	11am	one of the Bde Lewis Guns, Both guns were withdrawn about 11 am to German 1st Line having fired 750 rounds at German 3rd Line to prevent counterattack. Guns were now about 20 yds apart in the German 1st Line & the remainder of the day passed without event.	
	2/7/16	3:30am	About 3.30 am Guns stood to as Germans had commenced a bombing raid which was repulsed later by our own bombers,	
		6.0pm	rest of day passed without event until 6 pm when a shell exploded over one of the guns seriously wounding 2/Lt JINKS and SGT. GALLACHER and a gun number & Killing two other numbers after this guns held on until relieved by the 14th Bde M.G. Coy about 10 pm.	
	1/7/16	8.0am	Two guns under 2/Lt GREGG with another Coy of the K.O.Y.L.I. failed to get beyond our own front line trench. These guns took up defensive position on the flanks of the Infantry, and withdrew with them to our 2nd Line (TOBERMORY ST) again taking up flank defensive positions where they remained until relieved about 10 am	
	3/7/16		on the 3/7/16 when they joined the remainder of the Coy at AVELUY.	

T2134. Wt. W708—776. 500000. 4/15. Sir J. C. & S.

Instructions regarding War Diaries and Intelligence Summaries are contained in F. S. Regs., Part II. and the Staff Manual respectively. Title pages will be prepared in manuscript.

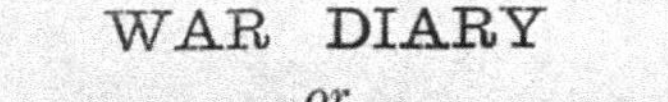

WAR DIARY
or
~~INTELLIGENCE~~ SUMMARY.

(Erase heading not required.)

Army Form C. 2118.

Place	Date	Hour	Summary of Events and Information	Remarks and references to Appendices
AUTHUILLE	1/7/16	8.0am	No 2 Sectn. Two guns under 2/Lt ELLISTON and two under 2/Lt LAVENDER attached to two Coys of the XI Borders left AUTHUILLE WOOD trenches about 8.0 am. and 2/Lt LAVENDER was wounded in the thigh before clearing the wood. Both parties came under a terrific machine gun fire the moment they left the wood 2/Lt. L's guns reached our second line with only 7 men under a Sergt. and Corpl & eventually the first line with 4 men, one gun was put out of action with shrapnel & the other mounted on the 1st line parapet, this gun never fired owing to not having a suitable target. 2/Lt ELLISTON reached our 1st line with only 1 gun and four men, this gun he installed in the parapet but did not fire owing to lack of target. This gun got into touch with the other which was about 30 yds to their right. Both guns hung on until ✱ ~~[illegible]~~	✱ compelled to retire owing to having insufficient gun numbers left uninjured, making it impossible to man the guns.
	1/7/16	2pm	about 2 pm & then withdrew to AVELUY. All casualties to No 2 Secn occurred between wood and our own 2nd Line.	

T2134. Wt. W708—776. 500000. 4/15. Sir J. C. & S.

Instructions regarding War Diaries and Intelligence Summaries are contained in F. S. Regs., Part II. and the Staff Manual respectively. Title pages will be prepared in manuscript.

WAR DIARY
or
~~INTELLIGENCE~~ SUMMARY.
(Erase heading not required.)

HEADQUARTERS No. .... Date .... 97th MACHINE GUN COY.

Army Form C. 2118.

Place	Date	Hour	Summary of Events and Information	Remarks and references to Appendices
UTHUILLE	1/7/16	4pm	No. 3 Section. At 4 pm. 7 men of this section were despatched to replace some men of No. 1 Sectn who had got detached from their	
		5.30pm	guns. At 5.30 pm. 2 gun teams under 2nd/Lt HANNAH were sent to KILBERRY ST & placed under the disposal of the O.C 16th H.L.I. They were there detailed to defend the British front line against an expected hostile raid. Lewis gun emplacements near SKINNER ST and KILMUR ST were occupied and nothing unusual happened	
	2/7/16	1.30	during the night. 1/2-7-6. At 1.30 am infantry were withdrawn to BISSET TRENCH, and the M.Gs remained in front line until	
		9.0am	9.0 am when they were also withdrawn to BISSET TRENCH. This	
	3/7/16	3.0am	position was retained until 3 am. when infantry were relieved by the 8th Border Regt. Guns were withdrawn to AVELUY at 4 pm	
	1/7/16		No 4. Sectn. The two guns under 2/Lt POWNALL from positions on CONNISTON HILL trench carried out intermittent fire on various parts of the LIEPSIG SALIENT during 1st-2nd-3rd July & from observation several assemblies of enemy troops behind the lines were	

T2134. Wt. W708–776. 500000. 4/15. Sir J. C. & S.

Instructions regarding War Diaries and Intelligence Summaries are contained in F. S. Regs., Part II. and the Staff Manual respectively. Title pages will be prepared in manuscript.

WAR DIARY
or
~~INTELLIGENCE SUMMARY.~~
(Erase heading not required.)

HEADQUARTERS No. .... Date .... 97th MACHINE GUN COY

Army Form C. 2118.

Place	Date	Hour	Summary of Events and Information	Remarks and references to Appendices
AUTHUILLE			dispersed by the fire of these guns. Owing to attack in the sector being held up the 2 guns of this section in reserve at LOMOND POST were not called upon. All guns withdrawn to AVELUY on 3/7/16	
	3/7/16			
AVELUY	3.7.16		All sections withdrawn from line and collected at AVELUY by about 2 pm. From here after a short rest and a good meal the Coy proceeded to billets at WARLOY where it spent the night.	
WARLOY	4.7.16		Draft of 30 men arrived from base about 2 am. Day was spent in checking section rolls, making casualty returns, equipment deficiency returns etc and generally reorganizing (Total gun casualties:— 1 lost in our own lines and 3 damaged)	
"	5.7.16		Morning spent in sending in indents & reorganization generally. In the afternoon Coy. removed to billets at HARPONVILLE arriving there about 7 pm.	
HARPONVILLE	6.7.16		Quiet day, very wet. Reorganization work carried on. Orders received to be ready to move at 1 hrs notice after 8 am on the 7th inst	
"	7.7.16		Still very wet. Company standing by all morning waiting for	

T2134. Wt. W708—776. 500000. 4/15. Sir J. C. & S.

Army Form C. 2118.

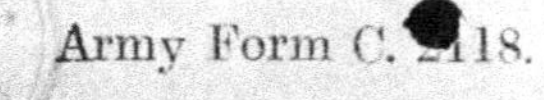

WAR DIARY
or
INTELLIGENCE SUMMARY.
(*Erase heading not required.*)

Instructions regarding War Diaries and Intelligence Summaries are contained in F. S. Regs., Part II. and the Staff Manual respectively. Title pages will be prepared in manuscript.

Place	Date	Hour	Summary of Events and Information	Remarks and references to Appendices
			movement orders, which were received at 3.30 pm. About 5 pm Coy moved to SENLIS where great difficulty was experienced in obtaining billets owing to the town being full. Orders were received here to be ready to proceed into the line at short notice. 2nd Lt E.S. ELLISTON evacuated to C.C.S (sick) and 2nd Lt A.S. GREAVES reported for duty from M.G. Base.	
SENLIS	8.7.16		At 9.15 pm the company moved into the line in the OVILLIERS sector to relieve the 33rd Bde M.G. Coy who had 8 guns in the line and 8 in reserve. The guns were placed with the view of worrying the enemy and at the same time defending the line. No.1. Section with 3 guns were put in reserve in dugouts in LUNE ST. No 2 Section not having yet received their new guns to replace those lost and damaged on the 1st inst were accomodated for the night in LUNE ST and returned to SENLIS on the 9th inst. No 3. Sectn put 2 guns in BURY AV. under 2nd Lt CRAVEN and 2 guns in defensive position in AUTHUILLE WOOD. No 4 Section placed 2 guns in LONGRIDGE ST and 2 guns in CONNISTON ST. This relief was completed by 4.30 am 9th inst. Transport returned to SENLIS.	

T2134. Wt. W708—776. 500000. 4/15. Sir J. C. & S.

Instructions regarding War Diaries and Intelligence Summaries are contained in F. S. Regs., Part II. and the Staff Manual respectively. Title pages will be prepared in manuscript.

WAR DIARY
or
~~INTELLIGENCE SUMMARY.~~
(Erase heading not required.)

Army Form C. 2118.

Place	Date	Hour	Summary of Events and Information	Remarks and references to Appendices
OVILLIERS SECTOR	9.7.16		The trenches were in a very muddy state. Two guns in CONNISTON ST. were laid on enemy communication trenches + opened fire on any movement being observed. these guns were in an excellent position looking down into the enemy trenches which were very much knocked about by our artillery so that any movement was easily detected. The 2 guns in LONGRIDGE ST had good positions but very poor emplacements the fire trenches and the Communication trenches being badly knocked about. Our dead from the offensive of July 1st had not all been collected which made it very bad for the men. It was found that the same field of fire could be obtained from CONNISTON ST. (which was in excellent order) so these 2 guns were put there at 7.30pm on the 9th And all four guns were then each alloted a certain portion of enemy trenches to cover. These guns were firing at intervals all day and night with apparently good results. Fire was chiefly directed into the NAB VALLEY	
	10.7.16		Firing only from the guns in CONNISTON ST. Not much enemy	

T2134. Wt. W708—776. 500000. 4/15. Sir J. C. & S.

Instructions regarding War Diaries and Intelligence Summaries are contained in F. S. Regs., Part II. and the Staff Manual respectively. Title pages will be prepared in manuscript.

WAR DIARY
or
~~INTELLIGENCE SUMMARY.~~
(Erase heading not required.)

Army Form C. 2118.

Place	Date	Hour	Summary of Events and Information	Remarks and references to Appendices
VILLIERS SECTOR			movement was observed, but a few targets were obtained & immediately fired on. Fine and dry	
	11.7.16		As on the 10th inst. At 7.30 pm an order was received through the Brigade from the Division ordering a gun to be placed in RIVINGTON SAP which had been dug across 'No Mans Land' and had been opened up as the impression was that we held the line at this point. This was found not to be the case so the sap was closed again and the guns sent to help to hold the sap. A trench mortar emplacement was converted into a M G emplacement. Weather bright and dry.	
	12.7.16		The 3 guns in CONNISTON St continued firing on enemy ration parties etc	
	13.7.16		As above, at 12 noon a party of about 50 Germans were fired on with apparently good results between R 32 C 3.1 and X.2. a.1.9. This was the largest party observed during present tour in trenches. 2Lt G MASTERS reported for duty from M.G Base.	X. 14.7.16 Reinforcement draft of 10 O.R. reported from M.G Base.
	14.7.16	X.	Firing as above. During the smoke barrage from 3.10am to 3.40 am	

T2134. Wt. W708—776. 500000. 4/15. Sir J. C. & S.

Instructions regarding War Diaries and Intelligence Summaries are contained in F. S. Regs., Part II. and the Staff Manual respectively. Title Pages will be prepared in manuscript.

WAR DIARY
or
~~INTELLIGENCE~~ SUMMARY
(Erase heading not required.)

Army Form C. 2118.

Place	Date	Hour	Summary of Events and Information	Remarks and references to Appendices
OVILLIERS SECTOR			the 2 guns in BURY AV. also opened fire, firing in the direction of MOQUET FARM. At 1 pm when our troops stood to + made a show of action in front line trenches; the two guns in BURY ST fired 16,000 rounds. between 3.10 am and 4 am and 1 pm and 1.30 pm. the guns in CONNISTON ST also fired continuously. The guns in RIVINGTON ST fired at intervals.	
	15.7.16		The Company was relieved by 4 guns of 146th Bde M.G. Coy. on left and 4 of 144th Bde M.G. Coy on the right, & proceeded to BOUZINCOURT where it was billeted for the night.	
BOUZINCOURT	16.7.16		No. 2 Section and transport joined the remainder of the Coy at BOUZINCOURT. At 3 pm. the Coy with the rest of the 97th Bde. left BOUZINCOURT and marched to AMPLIER where the night was spent.	
AMPLIER	17.7.16		Coy marched from AMPLIER to SUS ST. LEGER where it spent the night in billets. Weather wet.	
SUS ST LEGER	18.7.16		Coy. paraded under Section Officers & spent the day in straightening up.	
"	19.7.16		Coy moved off from SUS. ST. LEGER at 8.30 am + marched to TACHINCOURT arriving there at 3.30 pm. Weather dull & showery.	
TACHINCOURT.	20.7.16		Coy left TACHINCOURT at 10 am and marched to HUCLIER arriving there at 2 pm. Weather hot.	
HUCLIER	21.7.16		Coy. left HUCLIER at 7.0 am. & marched to ~~HUCLIE~~ ALLOUAGNE arriving there at 1.30 pm. Weather hot.	

2449 Wt. W14957/M90 750,000 1/16 J.B.C. & A. Forms/C.2118/12.

Instructions regarding War Diaries and Intelligence Summaries are contained in F. S. Regs., Part II. and the Staff Manual respectively. Title Pages will be prepared in manuscript.

WAR DIARY
or
INTELLIGENCE SUMMARY
(Erase heading not required.)

Army Form C. 2118.

Place	Date	Hour	Summary of Events and Information	Remarks and references to Appendices
ALLOUAGNE	22.7.16		Company paraded under section officers and straightened up generally. Weather fine	
"	23.7.16		Coy paraded at 10am under Section Officers. 2nd LT. J.M.F CRAVEN 1 SERGT 1 CPL. and 8 O.R. with 2 guns proceeded to FERFAY for the purpose of instructing Battn drafts in the VICKERS GUN. 1. VICKERS GUN and team sent to ~~LONGUAY~~ LAPUGNOY to protect Ordnance Depot there in case of aerial attack.	
"	24.7.16		Coy. paraded under Section Officers for ordinary routine work.	
"	25.7.16		do do to straighten up prior to vacating billets etc	
"	26.7.16		Coy. left ALLOUAGNE at 10am and marched to BETHUNE and arrived there at 2pm & took over billets in the town	
BETHUNE	27.7.16		Coy. paraded under Section Officers and refitting was carried on with only about 20% of the men being still left unfinished. Preparations were also made for the inspection by the G.O.C 1st Army Corps	
	28.7.16		97th Bde was inspected by General Sir Charles Monro, G.O.C First Army	
	29.7.16		Coy Paraded for fatigues & instruction under Section Officers.	
	30.7.16		Church parade at 2pm. 2/Lt J.M.F. Craven proceeded to join 9th Bn North'd Fusiliers	
	31.7.16		Coy paraded under Section Officers	

2449 Wt. W14957/M90 750,000 1/16 J.B.C. & A. Forms/C.2118/12.

97th Brigade.

32nd Division.

-9-----------

97th BRIGADE MACHINE GUN COMPANY

AUGUST 1 9 1 6

V016

Confidential

Volume VI

War Diary

of

97th Machine Gun Company

for the month of

August 1916.

from 1st August 1916 to 31st August 1916

W. A. Stanley Capt.
Commanding,
97 MACHINE GUN COY.

Army Form C. 2118.

Instructions regarding War Diaries and Intelligence Summaries are contained in F. S. Regs., Part II. and the Staff Manual respectively. Title Pages will be prepared in manuscript.

WAR DIARY
or
INTELLIGENCE SUMMARY
(Erase heading not required.)

Place	Date	Hour	Summary of Events and Information	Remarks and references to Appendices
BETHUNE	August 1		The morning was spent on Gun drill, physical training etc., in the afternoon the company went bathing.	
			No 8714 Pte Mason J.J. & 7869 Pte Edwards. D admitted to Hospital	W.A.G.
			" 7919 Sergt Stephenson J.H. rejoined from base. This N.C.O. had been sent to the base as being 'too slow' for a Machine Gunner	
"	2		The company paraded at 7.15 am for a route march returning at 10.30am. in the afternoon another bathing parade was held.	W.A.G.
			No 7928 Pte TURNER G. admitted to hospital	
"	3		The sections paraded under their Officers for drill etc.	W.A.G.
"	4		" " " " " " " & gun cleaning as orders were received to get ready for the line.	W.A.G.
			Capt STANLEY & 2nd Lieut POWNALL went to the CAMBRIN Sector to view the line & make arrangements for the relief. The A.D.V.S. gave a lecture to the drivers on "Horse Management	
		6.30pm 8.30pm	6 guns were sent to CAMBRIN & put in a cellar for the night in order to facilitate the relief on the 5th	
"	5	8.am	6 Gun Teams under 2nd Lts POWNALL, GREGG & MASTERS proceed to the CAMBRIN sector to relieve 5 guns of No 24 M.G. Coy & took up positions as shown on map 'A' positions 1 to 6	W.A.G.
"		10.15 am	Hd Qrs & remaining sections marched to billets in BEUVRY	

2449 Wt. W14957/M90 750,000 1/16 J.B.C. & A. Forms/C.2118/12.

Instructions regarding War Diaries and Intelligence Summaries are contained in F. S. Regs., Part II. and the Staff Manual respectively. Title Pages will be prepared in manuscript.

WAR DIARY
or
~~INTELLIGENCE SUMMARY~~
(Erase heading not required.)

Army Form C. 2118.

2

Place	Date	Hour	Summary of Events and Information	Remarks and references to Appendices
CAMBRIN	Aug 5	9.30pm	During the night No 1.2.4.5 & 6 guns fired in all 5250 rounds at the following targets :- A29 a 5.4 to A29 b 1.9 - A29 d - A29 b 4.5 A23 a 4.6 - A23 c 1.4 - A29 b 4.5. Enemy M.G. action also a few 77m shells over No 6 gun. 7863 Pte Dibbage a. admitted to Hospital. 7828 Pte Turner G & C.C.S.	WAS
	6	10.0am	The company ~~marched~~ (less the 1½ sections in the line) marched to BETHUNE to attend a Commemoration Service. Two more guns were sent up to the line & took up positions in RAILWAY KEEP to act as reserves & were only to be used in case of emergency	WAS
"		12.5am	All 6 guns fired during the night, expending 6250 rounds at the following targets (1) Road from ESTAMINET A29 a 5 4 to AUCHY (Transport was heard on this road, but was not silenced) (2) Cross roads A29 d 3 5 (3) A29 b 4 5 to A23 c 15.35 (4) A22 b 25.45 to A23 a 4 6 & (4) A23 c 6.6 (5) A29 b 4.5 (6) A23 c 85.15 to A29 b 1.9. Enemy M.G's were much more active than on previous night	
"		9.30pm		
"			The 2 gun teams returned from Divisional School at FERFAY & were billeted in BEUVRY. Lieut WALLACE & Sergt PARKER were retained at the school as instructors for the next course. The gun was also retained.	
	7		The sections in BEUVRY paraded under their section officers. The 6 guns in OLD BOOTS Trench fired in all 6000 rounds as targets as above. Transport was again heard of the AUCHY road & when fire was	WAS

Instructions regarding War Diaries and Intelligence Summaries are contained in F. S. Regs., Part II. and the Staff Manual respectively. Title Pages will be prepared in manuscript.

WAR DIARY
or
~~INTELLIGENCE SUMMARY~~
(Erase heading not required.)

Army Form C. 2118.

3

Place	Date	Hour	Summary of Events and Information	Remarks and references to Appendices
			opened the noise ceased. Enemy M.G's retaliated	
			No 27001 Pte SUNDERLAND.W. discharged Hospital	
	8		Sections in BEUVRY paraded under section Officers	
CAMBRIN			The guns in the line fired 6250 rounds at various targets, the enemys retaliation was very marked	WAS
	9		The sections in the line were relieved by the sections in BEUVRY. on relief the 2 sections went to billets in ANNEQUIN to act as reserves & be ready to move up at an hours notice.	WAS
"			Capt STANLEY & Headquarters moved to FACTORY TRENCH & established headquarters there. Quarter Masters stores & Transport remained at BEUVRY. 2nd Lieut POWNALL went back to be in charge of these details. 6250 rounds were fired during the night. Enemy M.G's active	
"	10		Orders were received for 3 guns to be put in the front line, as there were no emplacements for these, they had to be mounted on the parapet. These were placed in such a position to get fire on the whole of No mans land. The guns 1, 2, 4, 5 & 6 fired in all 4500 rounds on same targets as above, Enemy M.G. fire pratically nil. Lieut C.S.SMITH evacuated to C.C.S.	WAS
	9		No 3187. ARKILL A. & 26293 Pte GROOM.E. discharged Hospital Sentence on 7908 Pte BAMFORD A. confirmed. sentenced to 6 months imprisonment	WAS

2449 Wt. W14957/M90 750,000 1/16 J.B.C. & A. Forms/C.2118/12.

Army Form C. 2118.

Instructions regarding War Diaries and Intelligence Summaries are contained in F. S. Regs., Part II. and the Staff Manual respectively. Title Pages will be prepared in manuscript.

WAR DIARY
or
~~INTELLIGENCE SUMMARY~~
(Erase heading not required.)

4

Place	Date	Hour	Summary of Events and Information	Remarks and references to Appendices
	10		No. 8714 Pte MASON & 7869 EDWARDS discharged hospital	[illegible]
CAMBRIN	11		Guns fired as on the 10th expending 3750 rounds during the night. Enemy M.G's fairly active.	
			No. 14800 Pte BURTON. A Killed. No. 29809 L/c WILSON. C.T. wounded. These 2 casualties were caused by shell fire in the front line trench.	[illegible]
"			7907 Sergt HOGGIT. E. rejoined from Base (This NCO was wounded on July 1st) 7847 Cpl PARTRIDGE " " " (This NCO has been sent down as "too slow") no improvement was noticed on his return.	[illegible]
	12		Firing as previous night. Enemy fairly quiet. 7920 Pte TUCK A & 12443 Pte PUSEY G admitted to Hospital	
	13		The 3 gun teams in front line were relieved by 3 gun teams from ANNEQUIN. Firing as before. Enemy much more active especially around No. 1 gun which was firing at A29 a 1.9 to A23 c 4.4. 7881 Driver DOHERTY, 7717 DRIVER LANCESTER, ~~Driver~~ 8717 Pte HOUSE (groom) admitted to Hospital. 9849 Pte PAUL E sent to Base, being too young for active service. 2nd Lieut N.J. KERR 14th East Yorks R att M.G.C. reported from Base	[illegible]
	14		Firing as on previous nights, Enemy fairly active. Day sniping was carried out from an old trench, at AUCHY steel BRICKWORKS — various other targets.	[illegible]

Army Form C. 2118.

WAR DIARY
or
INTELLIGENCE SUMMARY
(Erase heading not required.)

Instructions regarding War Diaries and Intelligence Summaries are contained in F. S. Regs., Part II. and the Staff Manual respectively. Title Pages will be prepared in manuscript.

5

Place	Date	Hour	Summary of Events and Information	Remarks and references to Appendices
CAMBRIN	15		Day sniping & Night firing carried out as before Enemy fairly active 15113 Pt. EDEN. E. accidentally wounded. 8717 Driver LANCASTER discharged hospital	WAS
"	16		1000 rounds were fired by day & 6000 rounds by night. Enemy transport was heard & fire was directed on A29 a 5.4 vertically searched to A29 a 9.8 transport ceased & was not heard again. Enemy M.G's retaliated vigorously 8588 Pte MEAD H. – 27001 Pte SUNDERLAND W. Admitted to hospital.	WAS
"	17		750 rounds fired during the day, 4900 by night, enemy been fairly active, his M.G's were especially active firing in the direction of No 1 gun 2nd Lt F. R. CROCOMBE 3rd Oxford & Bucks L.I. att M.G.C. reported for duty from the base 7881 Pte DOHERTY. B. discharged hospital.	WAS
"	18		500 rounds were fired by day & 5750 by night on various targets the night was fairly quiet. No 7874 Driver ALLEN. G. – 7866 Driver GLAVEN P. Evacuated to C.C.S.	WAS
	19		750 rounds fired during the day 6000 by night at various targets Enemy was fairly active	WAS

2449 Wt. W14957/M90 750,000 1/16 J.B.C. & A. Forms/C.2118/12.

Army Form C. 2118.

6

WAR DIARY
or
~~INTELLIGENCE~~ SUMMARY

(Erase heading not required.)

Instructions regarding War Diaries and Intelligence Summaries are contained in F. S. Regs., Part II. and the Staff Manual respectively. Title Pages will be prepared in manuscript.

Place	Date	Hour	Summary of Events and Information	Remarks and references to Appendices
CAMBRIN	20		750 rounds were fired during the day & 4500 by night at various targets. Enemy retaliation nil during the night. 14887 Pte GROUNDLEM adm. Hosp. Transport & QM Stores moved to BETHUNE.	
	21		The 3 guns in the front line were relieved 2 guns at RAILWAY KEEP & No 1 gun all by No 96 company. On relief the teams proceeded to billets in BETHUNE. 2nd Lt T.W. GREGG & team proceed to LAPUGNOY to relieve a gun of No 96 company there	
CAMBRIN	21		500 rounds were fired by day & 4000 by night, enemy slightly more active. No 2 gun was relieved by No 96 company. The team when relieved proceeded to BETHUNE. 7899 Pte BARRON admitted to Hosp.	
	22		Firing as on the 21st. Orders were received at 9.30 pm that Commanding Officers were to proceed to the HULLUCH Sector on the 23rd to view the line. Capt Stanley left the trenches & proceeded to BETHUNE	
	23	9 am	6 gun teams proceeded to PHILOSOPHE & marched straight into the line relieving 6 guns of No 48 M.G. Coy in RESERVE TRENCH HULLUCH Sector. Company Head Quarters were established in PHILOSOPHE & the transport accommodated in NOEUX-LES-MINES The company was then distributed as follows –	

2449 Wt. W14957/M90 750,000 1/16 J.B.C. & A. Forms/C.2118/12.

Army Form C. 2118.

WAR DIARY
or
~~INTELLIGENCE SUMMARY~~
(Erase heading not required.)

Instructions regarding War Diaries and Intelligence Summaries are contained in F. S. Regs., Part II. and the Staff Manual respectively. Title Pages will be prepared in manuscript.

Place	Date	Hour	Summary of Events and Information	Remarks and references to Appendices
	23		4 guns in OLD BOOTS TRENCH CAMBRIN Sector under 2nd Lt HANNAM	
			4 guns in reserve in ANNEQUIN under 2nd Lt MASTERS	
			1 gun at LAPUGNOY under 2nd Lt GREGG	
			1 gun at FERFAY for instructional purposes (Lieut WALLACE here)	
			6 guns in RESERVE TRENCH HULLUCH Sector under 2nd Lts GREAVES KERR & CROCOMBE.	
			Transport & Q.M. Stores at NOEUX-LES-MINES under 2nd Lt POWNALL	
			Head quarters at PHILOSOPHE	
			3 guns in the HULLUCH Sector fired 6750 rounds during the night at various targets, enemy MG's very active	
			The guns in the CAMBRIN Sector fired as usual.	
	24		Company distributed as above, firing as on previous night, enemy less active than last night. 7508 L/c SEABORNE admitted to hospital.	
	25	9.30 AM	The 4 guns in the CAMBRIN Sector were relieved by No 96 M.G. Coy, on completion of relief this section marched to billets in PHILOSOPHE	
		10 AM	The 4 guns in ANNEQUIN were also relieved by 96 M.G. Coy & proceeded to PHILOSOPHE	
		2 pm	The gun at LAPUGNOY was relieved by No 2 Motor Machine Gun Battery	

2449 Wt. W14957/M90 750,000 1/16 J.B.C. & A. Forms/C.2118/12.

Army Form C. 2118.

8

Instructions regarding War Diaries and Intelligence Summaries are contained in F. S. Regs., Part II. and the Staff Manual respectively. Title Pages will be prepared in manuscript.

WAR DIARY
or
~~INTELLIGENCE SUMMARY~~
(Erase heading not required.)

Place	Date	Hour	Summary of Events and Information	Remarks and references to Appendices
	25		This gun team also proceeded to PHILOSOPHE on completion of relief. The guns in the HULLUCH Sector fired during the night as usual. Enemy M.G's were less active than previously.	W.A.G.
			5584 CSM. Savage evacuated to C.C.S.	
	26	1.30pm	5 guns (4 from ANNEQUIN + 1 from LAPUGNOY) relieved 5 guns of No 24 M.G. Coy. 3 in the VILLAGE LINE, 1 in PONT ST + 1 in POSSEN ALLEY, these were reserve positions & only to fire in case of emergency.	W.A.G.
			The ~~gun~~ Section at PHILOSOPHE spent the day putting the limbers in order & cleaning up generally.	
			4 guns in Reserve Trench fired during the night on various targets. Enemy M.G. fire practically nil.	
	27		Company distributed as above. 7,250 rounds were fired during the night by 4 guns. Enemy M.G. fire nil. 7879 Driver ~~Pte~~ RICHARDS G. evacuated to CCS suffering from injuries received by being thrown from a mule. 7920 Pte TUCK A discharged from hospital.	W.A.G.
	27		A Court of enquiry was held to enquire into the circumstances of the accident to Driver Richards.	W.A.G.
	28		Company distributed as above. Firing as on previous days.	W.A.G.

2449 Wt. W14957/M90 750,000 1/16 J.B.C. & A. Forms/C.2118/12.

Army Form C. 2118.

Instructions regarding War Diaries and Intelligence Summaries are contained in F. S. Regs., Part II. and the Staff Manual respectively. Title Pages will be prepared in manuscript.

WAR DIARY
or
INTELLIGENCE SUMMARY
(Erase heading not required.)

9

Place	Date	Hour	Summary of Events and Information	Remarks and references to Appendices
	29		Company distributed as above. During the afternoon a bombardment, which had been prearranged, took place at 4.20 pm. 4 guns which had been removed to open emplacements in disused trenches took part in this by firing on enemy communication trenches & HULLUCH main road. These guns fired for 4 minutes in all firing 5,000 rounds in all. Firing was carried out during the night as usual.	WAS
	30	4 pm	No 8 M.G. Coy commenced to relieve the guns in the line. This relief was completed at 8.15 pm. The company marched back to BETHUNE & was billeted in the Orphanage.	WAS
BETHUNE	31	9.30am	The company paraded under section officers for gun cleaning & straightening up limbers generally.	WAS
		11.30am	One of the guns had been taken from the limber mounted on the tripod, ready for cleaning, the man pressed the thumb piece & the gun fired, the bullet hitting Pte WILLIAMS in the leg, seriously wounding him.	
		2 pm	A court of Enquiry assembled to enquire into the circumstances relating to the accidental wounding of Ptes EDEN & Pte WILLIAMS. 13088 Pte MORGAN. H reported from the Base as a re-inforcement.	

W A Stanley Capt
Comndg 97th Machine Gun Company

2449 Wt. W14957/M90 750,000 1/16 J.B.C. & A. Forms/C.2118/12.

97th Brigade.

32nd Division.

97th BRIGADE MACHINE GUN COMPANY

SEPTEMBER 1 9 1 6

Vol 7

97th Machine Gun Company.

Original

War Diary.

Volume VII

for September 1916.

W A Stanley Capt
Commanding.
97th MACHINE GUN COY.

HEADQUARTERS
No. C.S. 57.
Date 30.9.16
97th MACHINE GUN COY.

Headquarters
97th Infantry Brigade

Herewith VOL. VII ~~Duplicate~~ Original
War Diary for month
of September 1916.

[signature] Capt.
Commanding,
97th MACHINE GUN COY.

30.9.16 2.

97 MG Coy.
Will you please
cause the attached War Diary
to be signed at the end by
the officer who keeps the diary.
Please return early

[signature] Capt
Staff Capt 97 Bde

Instructions regarding War Diaries and Intelligence Summaries are contained in F. S. Regs., Part II. and the Staff Manual respectively. Title Pages will be prepared in manuscript.

Original

WAR DIARY
or
INTELLIGENCE SUMMARY
(Erase heading not required.)

Army Form C. 2118.

[illegible] Capt. Commanding 97. MACHINE GUN COY.

Place	Date	Hour	Summary of Events and Information	Remarks and references to Appendices
BETHUNE.	1.9.16	—	Company still in Rest Billets & paraded under Section Officers	
	2.9.16		As above. Lieut C. Sydney SMITH rejoined from Base Depot.	
	3.9.16		Fifty (50) N.C.Os & men went up to trenches under 2/Lts MASTERS & GREGG to fill sandbags for H.Q. dugout in CAMBRIN Sectn.	
	4.9.16		Party as above again went to trenches	
	5.9.16		Work commenced on permanent horse standings, the shale being carted from ANNEZIN.	
	6.9.16		Orders received to relieve 14th M.G Coy (11 guns) in the CUINCHY Sectn. The guns were sent up & dumped near the entrance to the communication trenches during the evening.	
LE PREOL (CUINCHY)	7.9.16		Nos 1, 2 & 3 Section left BETHUNE at 9.0 am & took over from the 14th M.G Coy as follows:— No. 1 Secn 4 guns on Right } Reserve line " 2 " 4 " in Centre } " 3 " 3 " on Left. } Relief was completed by 4 pm without any hitch. No 4 Secn & HQs left BETHUNE at 11 am with transport. The HQs & No 4 Secn going to LE PREOL & the transport lines were situated at LE QUESNOY.	See Map Appendix No. 1
	8.9.16		Guns & Section stated in the CUINCHY sector in the Reserve line & firing at targets mentioned in appendix A. Lieut E. L WALLACE rejoined Coy from Divisional School of Instruction FERFAY.	See Map & Appendix A.

2449 Wt. W14957/M90 750,000 1/16 J.B.C. & A. Forms/C.2118/12.

Instructions regarding War Diaries and Intelligence Summaries are contained in F. S. Regs., Part II. and the Staff Manual respectively. Title Pages will be prepared in manuscript.

WAR DIARY
or
INTELLIGENCE SUMMARY
(Erase heading not required.)

Army Form C. 2118.

HEADQUARTERS No. VOL. VII. 30.9.16 MACHINE GUN COY.

Capt. Commanding, 97. MACHINE GUN COY.

Place	Date	Hour	Summary of Events and Information	Remarks and references to Appendices
GUINCHY SECTOR	9.9.16	—	Company in trenches as above stated. 2nd Lt GREAVES with 3 guns & teams of No 4 Section moved into line & took over the VILLAGE defence lines. (One gun & team of No 3 ~~Trenches~~ Section sent up to 2/Lt HANNAH (O/C No 3 Sect) to occupy an additional emplacement. The Coy guns now fired intermittently throughout the night on the various targets & certain guns also fired during the day & the German M.G. fire was reported by the Battalion O/C's to have been considerably reduced in consequence. Work commenced on permanent horse standings at LEQUESNOY	See map
	10.9.16 11.9.16 12.9.16 13.9.16 14.9.16 15.9.16 16.9.16		Company in trenches as above stated. During the day time the Sections were kept busy improving the state of the trenches in their vicinity & the work of laying duckboards & revetting the sides & improving emplacements and dugouts ready for the winter was pushed on with every day. The guns maintained their nightly firing & received very little effective retaliation & no casualties.	
	17.9.16	—	The Artillery & Heavy T.M.S carried out a combined 'Strafe' on a point A.16.C.6.5 just north of the enemy's BRICKSTACKS where some works were in progress. The 'Strafe' took place at 3.15 pm & the F.O.P's reported a great amount of damage was done. During the evening 2/Lt HANNAH mounted a gun on the South side of the CANAL embankment to fire on this spot (A16.C.6.5) but he could not get satisfactory laying. So the gun was moved to our front line & a rough emplacement made in the parados of the trench from which the	

2449 Wt. W14957/M90 750,000 1/16 J.B.C. & A. Forms/C.2118/12.

Instructions regarding War Diaries and Intelligence Summaries are contained in F. S. Regs., Part II. and the Staff Manual respectively. Title Pages will be prepared in manuscript.

Army Form C. 2118.

WAR DIARY
or
INTELLIGENCE SUMMARY
(Erase heading not required.)

HEADQUARTERS No. VOL. VII Date 30.9.16 97th MACHINE GUN COY.

Capt Commanding 97 MACHINE GUN COY.

Place	Date	Hour	Summary of Events and Information	Remarks and references to Appendices
CUINCHY SECTOR	17.9.16	–	Gun got a perfect command of the point. The gun fired from this position throughout the night at a range of about 300 yds & did considerable execution among the Hun working parties endeavouring to repair the damage done in the afternoon by our Artillery	CH
	18.9.16	–	Very heavy rain continued throughout the day making the trenches in a very wet & muddy state	CH
	19.9.16	–	Trenches wet & weather still wet & unsettled. M.G.s opened rapid fire during the night in conjunction with the infantry. Retaliation feeble	CH
	20.9.16	–	Continuous day & night fire kept up. Enemy M.G.s very active	
		pm	about 6 pm. A heavy T.M. fell near the gun about	
	21.9.16		1.30 am. On the gun opening fire a few minutes later several T.Ms were sent over falling close to the emplacement. During the day gun was moved to a different emplacement.	CH
	22.9.16		Continuous night & day fire kept up. At 8.45 pm. transport was heard in direction of A.23 a 5.5. & was heard to rattle away when fire was opened on this spot by our M.G.s. At 10.[illegible] pm transport was again heard from direction of A.23.c. Continuous fire was opened & transport stopped. A. Aerial darts fired round this gun at 10.30 pm.	CH
	23.9.16		Continuous day & night fire. Retaliation very feeble.	CH

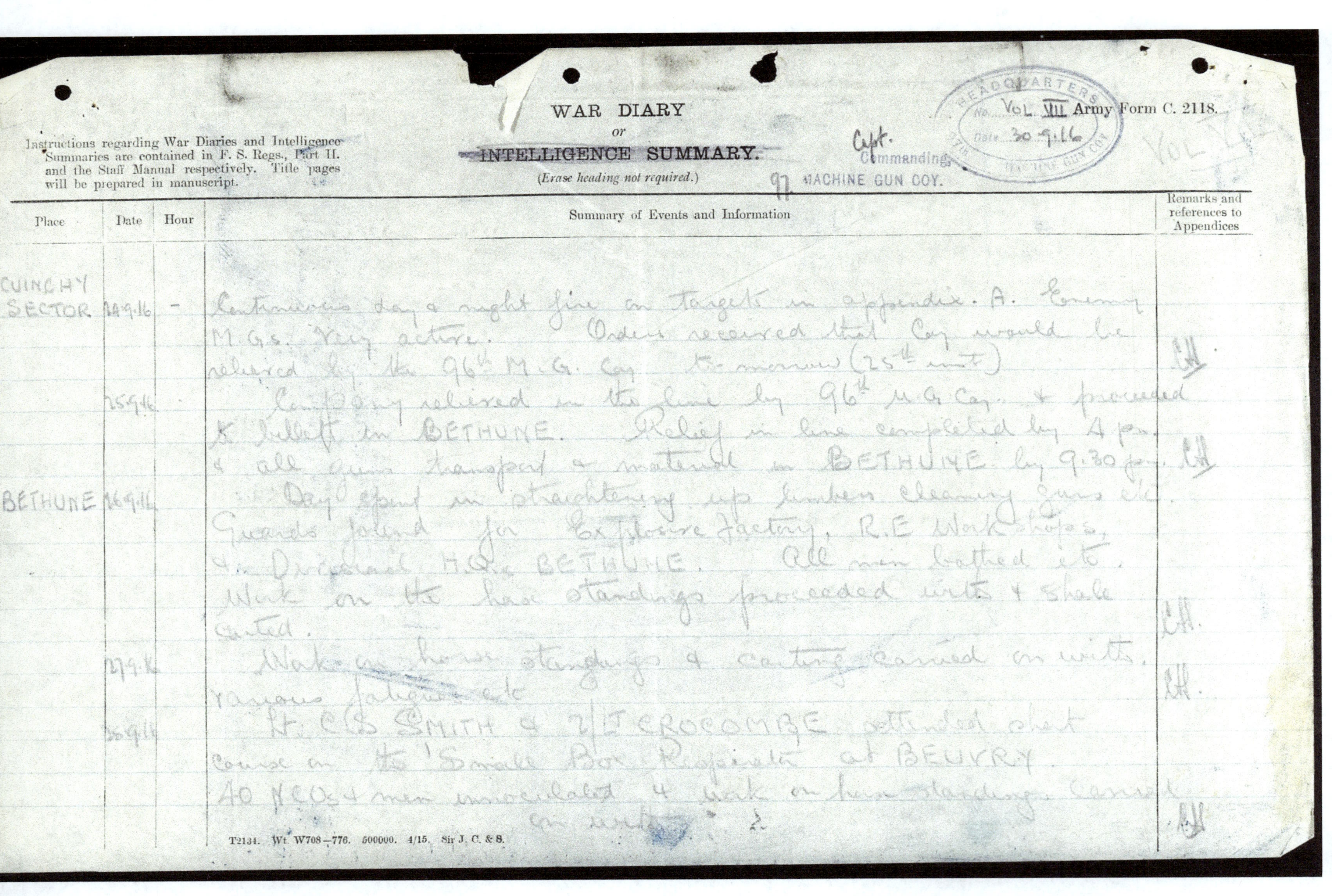

Instructions regarding War Diaries and Intelligence Summaries are contained in F. S. Regs., Part II. and the Staff Manual respectively. Title pages will be prepared in manuscript.

WAR DIARY
or
~~INTELLIGENCE SUMMARY.~~
(Erase heading not required.)

Army Form C. 2118.

HEADQUARTERS No. VOL. VII Date 30.9.16 97th MACHINE GUN COY.

Capt. Commanding 97 MACHINE GUN COY.

Place	Date	Hour	Summary of Events and Information	Remarks and references to Appendices
CUINCHY SECTOR	24.9.16	–	Continuous day & night fire on targets in appendix. A. Enemy M.G.s. very active. Orders received that Coy would be relieved by the 96th M.G. Coy tomorrow (25th inst)	
	25.9.16		Company relieved in the line by 96th M.G. Coy. & proceeded to billets in BETHUNE. Relief in line completed by 4 pm. & all guns transport & material in BETHUNE by 9.30 pm.	
BETHUNE	26.9.16		Day spent in straightening up limbers cleaning guns etc. Guards found for Explosive Factory, R.E Workshops, & Divisional H.Q.s BETHUNE. All men bathed etc. Work on the [illegible] standings proceeded with & shale carted.	
	27.9.16		Work on horse standings & carting carried on with. Various fatigues etc	
	28.9.16		Lt. C.S. SMITH & 2/Lt CROCOMBE attended short course on the 'Small Box Respirator' at BEUVRY. 40 N.C.Os & men inoculated & work on horse standings carried on with.	

T2134. Wt. W708—776. 500000. 4/15. Sir J. C. & S.

Instructions regarding War Diaries and Intelligence Summaries are contained in F. S. Regs., Part II. and the Staff Manual respectively. Title Pages will be prepared in manuscript.

WAR DIARY
or
INTELLIGENCE SUMMARY
(Erase heading not required.)

Army Form C. 2118.

Vol. VI

Place	Date	Hour	Summary of Events and Information	Remarks and references to Appendices
BETHUNE	29.9.16	-	Work in horse standings proceeded with. 2/Lt M.L.S. POWNALL proceeded to U.K. on leave	CH
	30.9.16		Coy. working in horse standings + various fatigues	CH

A. Sydney Smith 2/Lt

Capt.
Commanding,
97. MACHINE GUN COY.

2449 Wt. W14957/M90 750,000 1/16 J.B.C. & A. Forms/C.2118/12.

Appendix A.

List of Targets

1. Main CAMBRIN - LE FAUBERG Road
2. Tow path on South bank of canal
3. Cross roads A23a35.70 and roads running N & S. from here
4. Track running from dump at A23a 34.95. to A23 a 0.9. and thence to A23 a1.7.
5. House (probably Bn Hq) A23a 55.95 and road leading to it.
6. Track running from A22b 1.65 to road A22b65.6
7. Communication Trench running through A23c
8. CHATEAU ALLEY.
9. MILL ALLEY.
10. Track running from A29 a 5.3 to A29 c4.8.
11. CANAL ALLEY
12. A17d Swinging traverse and vertical search
13. A 18c
14. A 23b
15. A 24a

Day Targets 1, 2, 3, 5, & 10

W A Stanley Capt
Commanding,
97. MACHINE GUN COY.

Cuinchy
Cambrin
Auchy
lez-la-Bassée
Haisnes
Cité
de Douvrin
Brickstacks
Brick Works
Brickfields
Fosse 6 de Haisnes
Fosse Nº 8
de Béthune
Corons de
Pékin
Maison
Rouge
Quarry
Distillery
Station
Lock
Cemetery
Vert
Feuillage
Burbure
Braddell Castle
VILLAGE LINE
G.S., G.S 3194
Ordnance Survey 1916
WAR DIARY 97 M. G. Coy. VOL. 7.

97th Brigade.

32nd Division.

97th BRIGADE MACHINE GUN COMPANY

OCTOBER 1 9 1 6

Confidential

HEADQUARTERS
No.
Date 1-11-16
MACHINE GUN COY.

Original

War Diary of
94th Machine Gun Company
for the month of October 1916
Volume VIII

[illegible signature]
Commanding,
94th MACHINE GUN COY.

Army Form C. 2118.

WAR DIARY
or
~~INTELLIGENCE SUMMARY~~
(Erase heading not required.)

Instructions regarding War Diaries and Intelligence Summaries are contained in F. S. Regs., Part II. and the Staff Manual respectively. Title Pages will be prepared in manuscript.

Place	Date	Hour	Summary of Events and Information	Remarks and references to Appendices
BETHUNE.	1.10.16		Parades under Section Officers. 1 man admitted hospital –	M.S.
"	2.10.16		" " " " 2 " " "	M.S.
CAMBRIN	3.10.16		Company relieved the 14th M.G. Coy. in CAMBRIN Sector – Considerable Enemy Retaliation. Lieut C.S. SMITH struck off the strength of the Coy – Transferred to 167 Coy. Lieut M.C. DAVIDSON taken on strength of Coy, from 53rd M.G. Coy vice Lieut Smith – 1 man admitted hospital –	M.S.
CAMBRIN	4.10.16		Guns fired Continuously day & Night on Enemy positions – 2 men returned from Leave –	M.S.
"	5.10.16		Guns fired continuously – Enemy working party dispersed –	M.S.
"	6.10.16		Continuous firing – Retaliation Nil – 2/Lt A.S. GREAVES & 3 men admitted hospital –	M.S.
"	7.10.16		Continuous firing – 2 Reinforcements from Base – Sergt ELSE C. promoted A/C.S.M. vice SAVAGE –	M.S.
"	8.10.16		Enemy working party dispersed at 8 p.m –	M.S.
"	9.10.16		Continuous firing – Retaliation Nil –	M.S.

2449 Wt. W14957/M90 750,000 1/16 J.B.C. & A. Forms/C.2118/12.

Instructions regarding War Diaries and Intelligence Summaries are contained in F. S. Regs., Part II. and the Staff Manual respectively. Title Pages will be prepared in manuscript.

WAR DIARY ~~or~~ ~~INTELLIGENCE SUMMARY~~

(Erase heading not required.)

Place	Date	Hour	Summary of Events and Information	Remarks and references to Appendices
CAMBRIN	10.10.16		Continuous firing – 2/Lt POWNALL returned from leave – 1 man discharged hospital – 1 man admitted hospital – 3 Reinforcements from Base. Captain W.A. STANLEY went on leave –	MWD
"	11.10.16		Firing day & Night – 3 small enemy working parties were seen & fired at –	MWD
"	12.10.16		Continuous firing – No Retaliation – 2 men admitted hospital –	MWD
BETHUNE	13.10.16		~~Firing Continuous~~ – Company was relieved by 64th M.G.C. & went into billets in BETHUNE.	MWD
"	14.10.16		Parade under Section Officers – Work was carried out by 1 Section in CAMBRIN SECTOR – 1 man admitted hospital –	MWD
LABEUVRIERE	15.10.16		Company marched to LABEUVRIERE – 2 men Str. off Strength (To Base) 1 Man returned from Shoeing Course –	MWD
LA THIEULOYE	16.10.16		Company marched to LA THIEULOYE – 2/LT KERR M.J. & 2/LT MASTERS G. & 4 O.R. to M.G. Course CAMMIERS –	MWD

2449 Wt. W14957/M90 750,000 1/16 J.B.C. & A. Forms/C.2118/12.

Army Form C. 2118.

WAR DIARY
or
~~INTELLIGENCE SUMMARY~~

(Erase heading not required.)

Instructions regarding War Diaries and Intelligence Summaries are contained in F. S. Regs., Part II. and the Staff Manual respectively. Title Pages will be prepared in manuscript.

Place	Date	Hour	Summary of Events and Information	Remarks and references to Appendices
SERICOURT	17.10.16		Company marched to SERICOURT – It carried out an Outpost scheme with the Bde. on the way –	[initials]
LONGVILLETTE	18.10.16		Company marched to LONGUEVILLETTE – 6 men admitted hospital	[initials]
"	19.10.16		Company marched half way to RUBEMBRE & then returned to LONGUEVILLETTE – 1 man adm. hosp. 1 man Evac. C.C.S. 2 men str. off. Strength – Reinforcements (1 Transport Sgt. 1 man) from Base	[initials]
"	20.10.16		Company paraded under Section officers – Capt. W.A. STANLEY returned from Leave – 1 man discharged hospital –	[initials]
RUBEMPRÉ	21.10.16		Company marched to RUBEMPRE –	[initials]
"	22.10.16		Paraded for Training under Section Officers 1 man Evac. C.C.S	[initials]
BOUZINCOURT	23.10.16		Company marched to BOUZINCOURT & went into Camp –	[initials]
"	24.10.16		Section Parades – 3 N.C.O.s to G.H.Q. School BLENDEQUES str. off Strength –	[initials]

2449 Wt. W14957/M90 750,000 1/16 J.B.C. & A. Forms/C.2118/12.

Army Form C. 2118.

Instructions regarding War Diaries and Intelligence Summaries are contained in F. S. Regs., Part II. and the Staff Manual respectively. Title Pages will be prepared in manuscript.

WAR DIARY
or
~~INTELLIGENCE~~ SUMMARY

(Erase heading not required.)

Place	Date	Hour	Summary of Events and Information	Remarks and references to Appendices
BOUZINCOURT	25.10.16		Parades under section officers – 3 men struck off the strength	MCD
"	26.10.16		Company carried out tactical Training under section officers – 1 man discharged from hospital –	MCD
"	27.10.16		Parades under section officers – 1 man went on Leave –	MCD
"	28.10.16		" " " " – 1 man adm. Hospital – 2 N.C.O. returned from Segregation Camp –	MCD
"	29.10.16		2/LIEUT N. PICKTHALL reported for duty from the Base –	MCD
RUBEMPRE	30.10.16		The Company marched to RUBEMPRE –	MCD
VAL-DE-MAISON	31.10.16		The Company marched to VAL-DE-MAISON –	MCD

In the Field
31-10-16

W A Stanley Capt
Comm'd[g] 97th Machine Gun Coy

2449 Wt. W14957/M90 750,000 1/16 J.B.C. & A. Forms/C.2118/12.

97th Brigade.

32nd Division.

97th BRIGADE MACHINE GUN COMPANY

NOVEMBER 1 9 1 6

Confidential

War Diary of

97th Machine Gun Company

for the month of

November 1916.

Volume ~~Folio~~ No IX

Vol 9

[signature] Capt.
Commanding,
97th MACHINE GUN COY.

Army Form

WAR DIARY
or
~~INTELLIGENCE SUMMARY~~

(Erase heading not required.)

94th Machine Gun Coy

Instructions regarding War Diaries and Intelligence Summaries are contained in F. S. Regs., Part II. and the Staff Manual respectively. Title Pages will be prepared in manuscript.

Place	Date	Hour	Summary of Events and Information	Remarks and references to Appendices
VAL-DE-MAISON	1/11/16		Company Paraded under Section Officers	[initials]
"	2/11/16		Company took part part in Brigade Training. 1 man proceeded on a Course of Cold shoeing at Abbeville. 1 attd. man Returned to Unit (2nd K.O.Y.L.I.)	[initials]
"	3/11/16		Training under Section Officers. 1 man discharged from hospital	[initials]
"	4/11/16		Tactical Training under the C.O. Lt. Wallace proceeded to join 53 M.G.C. as 2nd in C.	[initials]
"	5/11/16		Physical Training & Tactical training. 2/Lt Pickthall, 1 N.C.O. & 1 man proceeded to M.G. Course CAMIERS	[initials]
"	6/11/16		2/Lt KERR & 2/Lt Masters, 2 N.C.O's & 2 men returned from M.G. School CAMIERS. 1 man admitted hospital. The Company took part in Brigade Training.	[initials]
"	7/11/16		Parade under Section Officers. 8 men (Reinforcements) reported from M.G. Base.	[initials]

Army Form C. 2118.

Instructions regarding War Diaries and Intelligence Summaries are contained in F. S. Regs., Part II. and the Staff Manual respectively. Title Pages will be prepared in manuscript.

WAR DIARY
or
~~INTELLIGENCE SUMMARY~~
(Erase heading not required.)

99th Machine Gun Coy.

Place	Date	Hour	Summary of Events and Information	Remarks and references to Appendices
VAL-DE-MAISON	8/11/16		Company paraded under Section Officers 2 O.R. discharged hospital –	M.W.D.
"	9/11/16		Company paraded ~~and~~ for Tactical Training – 1 N.C.O admitted hospital	M.W.D.
"	10/11/16		Parades under Section Officers –	M.W.D.
"	11/11/16		Company paraded for Route March – 2 men from 17th H.L.I. 4 from 16th H.L.I. 4 from 11th Borders 2 from 2nd K.O.Y.L.I. reported for duty with the Company – 1 man admitted hospital –	M.W.D.
"	12/11/16		Company attended Church Service with 17th H.L.I.	M.W.D.
CONTAY –	13/11/16		The Company moved to Billets in CONTAY – Two Men proceeded on Leave to U.K. Two Men transferred to Heavy Section M.G.C.	M.W.D.
MARTINSART	14/11/16		Company moved to Billets in MARTINSART – 1 N.C.O Transferred to Heavy Section M.G.C. 1 N.C.O adm. Hospital – Two Men reported from M.G.C. Base Depot.	M.W.D.
~~14/11/16~~ ENGLEBELMER	15/11/16		Company moved to ENGLEBELMER – 1 man discd. Hospital –	M.W.D.
"	16/11/16		Company paraded for getting guns etc. ready for Action –	M.W.D.

2449 Wt. W14957/M90 750,000 1/16 J.B.C. & A. Forms/C.2118/12.

Army Form C. 2118.

WAR DIARY
or
~~INTELLIGENCE SUMMARY~~ 94th Machine Gun Coy

(*Erase heading not required.*)

Instructions regarding War Diaries and Intelligence Summaries are contained in F. S. Regs., Part II. and the Staff Manual respectively. Title Pages will be prepared in manuscript.

Place	Date	Hour	Summary of Events and Information	Remarks and references to Appendices
TRENCHES. W. of BEAUMONT-HAMEL.	17/11/16		The Company took over gun positions in Sector N. of BEAUMONT-HAMEL from 112th M.G.C. and 154th M.G.C.	McA
"	18/11/16		The Company assisted 97th Bde in an attack on Enemy positions in MUNICH + FRANKFORT TRENCHES (see attached appendix) In this Action 2/LT KERR N.J. was wounded, 2/LT HANNAH W. was wounded, remaining at duty, 10 O.R. were killed. 16 O.R. wounded, 4 O.R. Missing.	McA.
ENGLEBELMER	19/11/16		The Company was relieved by 96th M.G.C. + returned to Billets in ENGLEBELMER.	McA
"	20/11/16		The Company paraded for cleaning guns + equipment. 1 man returned from Leave.	McA
MAILLY-MAILLET	21/11/16		Company moved to MAILLY-MAILLET. 1 man admitted Hosp. 1 driver reported from A.H.T.D.	McA
"	22/11/16		Company paraded for inspection by G.O.C. Res. Army. ~~[illegible]~~	McA
RAINCHEVAL	23/11/16		Company moved to billets in RAINCHEVAL. 5 men reported from M.G.C. Base Depot. 1 man ~~admitt~~ disch. Hosp.	McA

Instructions regarding War Diaries and Intelligence Summaries are contained in F. S. Regs., Part II. and the Staff Manual respectively. Title pages will be prepared in manuscript.

WAR DIARY
or
~~INTELLIGENCE SUMMARY.~~
(Erase heading not required.)

Army Form C. 2118.

97th Machine Gun Coy

Place	Date	Hour	Summary of Events and Information	Remarks and references to Appendices
BAINCHEVAL	24/11/16		The day was devoted to cleaning clothing, arms etc.	MA
BEAUVAL	25/11/16		The Company moved to billets in BEAUVAL – 1 Reinforcement reported from Base Depot	MA
BERTEAUCOURT	26/11/16		The Company moved to billets in BERTEAUCOURT –	MA
"	27/11/16		The day was devoted to cleaning clothing, arms, animals & wagons – 2/Lt M PICKTHALL, 1 N.C.O & 1 man rejoined from M.G. School, Base – 1 man adm. hospital, 1 man disch. hospital – 1 N.C.O proceeded on Leave – 1 man returned from Leave – 3 men reported from ~~Base~~ 11th Border Regt & taken on strength –	MA
"	28/11/16		As for 27/11/16 – 1 man admitted hospital 1 N.C.O proceeded to Base Depot & struck off strength (Auth. A.G. 6864 dated 23/10/16 & 37280 dated 25/11/16) 2 men admitted hospital –	MA
"	29/11/16		Company paraded for Physical Training & Squad Drill – Baths in afternoon – 2/Lt Matson proceeded on leave – 1 N.C.O rejoined from hospital – Sergt. Martin No. 5 M.G.C. reported for duty as C.S.M. and taken on strength –	MA
	30/11/16		Parades for P.T. & drill – Recreational Training in afternoon –	MA

W.A. Stanley Capt.
Commdg 97th M.G. Coy

T2134. Wt. W708–776. 500000. 4/15. Sir J. C. & S.

Instructions regarding War Diaries and Intelligence Summaries are contained in F. S. Regs., Part II. and the Staff Manual respectively. Title pages will be prepared in manuscript.

WAR DIARY
or
~~INTELLIGENCE SUMMARY.~~
(Erase heading not required.)

Army Form C. 2118.

94th Machine Gun Coy

Place	Date	Hour	Summary of Events and Information	Remarks and references to Appendices
			APPENDIX to ENTRIES dated 17/11/16, 18/11/16 19/11/16.	
			ACTION of COMPANY during OPERATIONS on above dates	
			ACTION of NO I SECTION –	
			No 1. Section paraded at 2.45 p.m on the 17/11/16 under 2/Lt POWNALL M.G.S. & marched to MAILLY-MAILLET where it joined the 16th H.L.I. to which it was attached for further operations. No 1. Gunteam under 2/Lt POWNALL was attached to A Coy. 16th H.L.I., No 2 Gun Team, having lost its way, reported to O.C. Coy. at Bde H.Q. where it was kept in Reserve – A Coy. moved to it's position in WAGON ROAD via WHITE CITY & CRATER TR. arriving at 3 a.m 18/11/16 – Shortly before 6 a.m. the 16th H.L.I. moved into position for the attack on MUNICH & FRANKFORT Trenches – No 1. Gun Team took up a position on the extreme right of the 16th H.L.I. – No 3 Section with 11th BORDER REGT was on the left and No 2 Section with 17th H.L.I on the right – At 6.10 a.m. the attack commenced No 1. Gun Team following the 3rd WAVE. On reaching NEW MUNICH TR. (the British Front Line) a gap occurred between the 16th & 17th H.L.I. – The Gun was placed in position, but it was considered expedient to push the gun forward, to give better protection to the infantry – A position was selected in a shellhole about 15 yards from	

T2134. Wt. W708–776. 500000. 4/15. Sir J. C. & S.

Instructions regarding War Diaries and Intelligence Summaries are contained in F. S. Regs., Part II. and the Staff Manual respectively. Title pages will be prepared in manuscript.

WAR DIARY
or
INTELLIGENCE SUMMARY.
(Erase heading not required.)

Army Form C. 2118.

94th Machine Gun Coy

Place	Date	Hour	Summary of Events and Information	Remarks and references to Appendices
			the German Front Line, MUNICH TR. – The position was consolidated & the gun placed ready for action – It was impossible to open fire owing to the position of our troops not being known – It was reported that a small portion of MUNICH TRENCH to the immediate front was still occupied by the enemy so the gun remained in position for an hour, being so placed to cover the retirement of small parties of the 16th H.L.I. & 17th H.L.I. who were retiring to NEW MUNICH TR. The gun then retired to NEW MUNICH TR. and was mounted in readiness for action – At 2.30 pm. acting under the orders of O.C. 16th H.L.I. the gun was withdrawn to WAGGON RD. and in conjunction with Nos. 3 & 2 Sections a defence of this line was arranged. The retirement of the gun team was rendered extremely difficult owing to heavy M.G. & Snipers fire – The position in WAGON RD. came under heavy shell fire during the night 18th/19th and the 19/11/16 – At 5.30 pm 19/11/16 the section was relieved by 96th M.G.C. & returned to Billets in ENGLEBELMER arriving at 10.30 pm	

T2131. Wt. W708–776. 500000. 4/15. Sir J. C. & S.

Instructions regarding War Diaries and Intelligence Summaries are contained in F. S. Regs., Part II. and the Staff Manual respectively. Title pages will be prepared in manuscript.

WAR DIARY
or
~~INTELLIGENCE~~ SUMMARY.
(Erase heading not required.)

Army Form C. 2118.

94th Machine Gun Coy

Place	Date	Hour	Summary of Events and Information	Remarks and references to Appendices
			ACTION of NO 2 SECTION–	
			On 17/11/16 No 2 Section under 2/Lt F.R. CROCOMBE moved up to WAGON ROAD– via BEAUMONT HAMEL – Two guns under 2/Lt MASTERS took over positions from 154th M.G.C. in LEAVE AVENUE, while the Remaining two guns under 2/Lt CROCOMBE remained in Reserve in WAGON ROAD– At 5.30 a.m. on 18/11/16. He moved his two guns up WAGON RD. to the end of LEAVE AV. + leaving them under cover there, went forward to learn the progress of the attack– He found that the 17th H.L.I. had not been able to consolidate MUNICH TR. and that consequently the guns under 2/Lt MASTERS had not gone forward– As there appeared to be only a few men left in the Trench, He moved up his two guns to LEAVE AV. to hold the trench– He then reported to O.C. 17th H.L.I. who confirmed this action– The Officer holding this sector desired one gun to be placed in NEW MUNICH TRENCH– This was done– While here a piece of shell struck a bag of bombs + exploded them, killing two men of the gun Team– AT. 10.30 a.m. 19th, THE SECTION was ordered to leave the trench, owing to a bombardment and on reaching WAGON ~~TR~~ RD. it met a relief from 96 M.G.C.	
			In the Evening it returned to billets in ENGLEBELMER.	

Instructions regarding War Diaries and Intelligence Summaries are contained in F. S. Regs., Part II. and the Staff Manual respectively. Title pages will be prepared in manuscript.

WAR DIARY
or
~~INTELLIGENCE SUMMARY.~~
(Erase heading not required.)

Army Form C. 2118.

97th Machine Gun Coy

Place	Date	Hour	Summary of Events and Information	Remarks and references to Appendices
			ACTION of NO 3 SECTION	
			The Section paraded under 2/Lt W. HANNAH at 11.30 p.m 16/11/16 in ENGLEBELMER and marched ~~to~~ via MAILLY-MAILLET to WHITE-CITY thence to position occupied by 112th M.G.C. 2 guns were in Strong pt. at Q5 c 26, one at Q6 617 and one in Reserve at Q5 a 76. No 4 Sect were on the Right and communication was established with them at 6 a.m. 17/11/16, and Crossfire arranged by both sections between WAGON ROAD and BEAUMONT TRENCH. All positions were heavily shelled between 6 p.m and 10 p.m. on 17/11/16 and gun at Q5 a 76 was knocked out & one man was killed. At the position in the Strong Pt one Sergt & 2 men were wounded. The remaining three teams evacuated positions at 3 a.m. 18/11/16 and reported to O.C. 11th BORDER REGT. at 4 a.m. at Q5 b 75.	
			Two guns one on each flank were to move forward with the last wave, the third was kept in reserve. SERGT STEPHENSON took forward the Left gun and suffered heavy Casualties,	

T2134. Wt. W708–776. 500000. 4/15. Sir J. C. & S.

Instructions regarding War Diaries and Intelligence Summaries are contained in F. S. Regs., Part II. and the Staff Manual respectively. Title pages will be prepared in manuscript.

WAR DIARY
or
INTELLIGENCE SUMMARY.
(Erase heading not required.)

Army Form C. 2118.

94th Machine Gun Coy

Place	Date	Hour	Summary of Events and Information	Remarks and references to Appendices
			he himself being wounded, so no information is available regarding his action — the gun on the Right, advanced along CRATER TRENCH to within 70 yds of MUNICH TR. where some successful firing was carried out against enemy snipers lining MUNICH TR. on the left, but the position became untenable owing to the enemy bombing down the communication Trench — Many stoppages occurred with the gun, the bad weather conditions having affected the Mechanism — This team retired on to WAGON ROAD, and with Reserve gun took up a position to cover ground to left of ROAD from CRATER TRENCH — at 3 p.m. 18/11/16 communication was established with No 4 Section on Left and at 3 a.m. 19/11/16 with No 1 Sect. on Right — No alteration in the situation occurred until 6.15 p.m. when orders were received to withdraw to WHITE CITY — Having reported there to O.C. Coy, at 8.30 p.m. the section returned to billets at ENGLEBELMER — The casualties incurred by this section were: 1 man killed, two N.C.Os and 2 men wounded — 3 men Missing —	

T2134. Wt. W708—776. 500000. 4/15. Sir J. C. & S.

Instructions regarding War Diaries and Intelligence Summaries are contained in F. S. Regs., Part II. and the Staff Manual respectively. Title pages will be prepared in manuscript.

WAR DIARY
or
~~INTELLIGENCE~~ ~~SUMMARY.~~
(Erase heading not required.)

Army Form C. 2118.

97th Machine Gun Coy

Place	Date	Hour	Summary of Events and Information	Remarks and references to Appendices
			ACTION of No 4 SECTION –	
			The section moved up, under 2/LT N. J. KERR, on the night of 16/11/16 via MAILLY-MAILLET, and relieved 4 guns of 112th Coy. Two guns took up positions at Q5 6 35, one at Q5 6 17 and one at Q5 6 41 – The positions were heavily shelled during the 17/11/16 – At 4.30 a.m 18/11/16 3 guns (CORP. PARTRIDGE's TEAM did not report) moved up WAGON ROAD TO K35 d 94 and took up positions with 2nd K.O.Y.L.I. – O.C. 2nd K.O.Y.L.I. ordered 2/LT KERR to advance with the 2nd wave moving ½ Left – The infantry however moved ½ Right and the section got left ~~[illegible]~~ on the left Flank – As soon as the advance commenced 2 men were killed by Snipers – When the Section had advanced about 15 yards, a number of Germans in a strong point at K36 c 15 held up their hands & 2/Lt KERR immediately went forward, hoping to rally some of the 2nd K.O.Y.L.I. who had hesitated, taking with him one Gun team. – When the Infantry did not	

T2131. Wt. W708–776. 500000. 4/15. Sir J. C. & S.

Army Form C. 2118.

WAR DIARY
or
INTELLIGENCE SUMMARY.
(Erase heading not required.)

97 Machine Gun Coy

Instructions regarding War Diaries and Intelligence Summaries are contained in F. S. Regs., Part II. and the Staff Manual respectively. Title pages will be prepared in manuscript.

Place	Date	Hour	Summary of Events and Information	Remarks and references to Appendices
			come on the enemy lay down, and 2/Lt KERR was shot through the head. Also one man was killed. This occurred at 7.25 a.m. 2/Lt KERR was subsequently brought in by an officer of the 2nd K.O.Y.L.I. wounded. SERGT. HALL then took command of the section. Finding the wire not cut, he found a small trench on his right. He placed his guns in position here. He held on as long as he could, but was enfiladed by shell and M.G. fire, and retired to WAGON ROAD & took up position there with one gun. One gun had been knocked out and the third had not arrived. SERGT HALL reported himself to 2/Lt HANNAH of No 3 Sect. He remained in WAGON RD. until ordered to withdraw to WHITECITY at 9.30 p.m 19/11/16. He brought back 3 guns which returned to Billets in ENGLEBELMER. The Section incurred casualties: 2/Lt KERR wounded. 3 men killed. 2 N.C.O.s 4 men wounded.	

W W Stanley Capt
Comm'd 97 M G Coy

T2134. Wt. W708—776. 500000. 4/15. Sir J. C. & S.

97th Brigade.

32nd Division.

97th BRIGADE MACHINE GUN COMPANY

DECEMBER 1 9 1 6

Vol 10

Confidential

97th Machine Gun Company.

War Diary for month

of

December

Volume X

2-1-17

W.A. Stanley Capt
Commdg.
97th M.G. Coy.

and the Staff Manual respectively. Title pages will be prepared in manuscript.

~~INTELLIGENCE SUMMARY.~~

(Erase heading not required.)

Place	Date	Hour	Summary of Events and Information	Remarks and references to Appendices
BERTEAUCOURT	1/12/16		Company paraded for Physical Training and Elementary Training under Section Officers – Recreational Training in afternoon.	[initials]
"	2/12/16		Company paraded for Route March – The Transport was inspected by G.O.C. Bde –	[initials]
"	3/12/16		Company inspected by C.O. and attended Church Parade – 1 man rejoined from hospital, & one man went on leave –	[initials]
"	4/12/16		Gun drill and Mechanism under Section Officers – Work was done on new Transport lines – Recr. Train.	[initials]
"	5/12/16		Company paraded for Firing on Range – Recr. Train.	[initials]
"	6/12/16		Company attended Bde Bombing Course – 2/Lt A.M. HUMBLE reported from M.G. Base Depot – Recreational Training Recreational Training in the afternoon – 1 man went on leave.	[initials]
"	7/12/16		Company paraded for Route March –	[initials]
"	8/12/16		" " under Section officers – 3 officers & 12 N.C.O's attended Bde. Physical Training Course – 1 man admitted hospital – 1 man rejoined from hosp.	[initials]

2353 Wt. W2544/1454 700,000 5/15 D. D. & L. A.D.S.S./Forms/C. 2118.

Instructions regarding War Diaries and Intelligence Summaries are contained in F. S. Regs., Part II. and the Staff Manual respectively. Title pages will be prepared in manuscript.

~~INTELLIGENCE SUMMARY.~~

(Erase heading not required.)

Place	Date	Hour	Summary of Events and Information	Remarks and references to Appendices
BERTEAUCOURT	9/12/16		Company paraded for P.T. and Musketry – 1 N.C.O + 1 man returned from leave – Recr. Train.	MRS
"	10/12/16		Company attended Church Parade	MRS
"	11/12/16		Company was inspected by G.O.C. V Corps – 21 men reported from M.G. Base Depot. 1 man adm. hospital	MRS.
"	12/12/16		Company paraded for M.G. Firing – Recr. Train –	MRS
"	13/12/16		" " " Route March – 3 officers + 12 N.C.O's attended Bde Physical Training Course – ~~1 officer~~ 2/Lt G. MASTERS returned from leave (12/12/16) 1 man went on leave.	MRS
"	14/12/16		Training under Section Officers – Recr. Train.	MRS
"	15/12/16		Company paraded for Bombing (Bde Course) 2 men returned from leave – 1 man adm. hosp.	MRS.
RUBEMPRE	16/12/16		The Company marched to billets in RUBEMPRE. 2 men went on Leave. 2/Lt CROCOMBE + 1 man returned from M.G. School CAMIERS –	MRS.

2353 Wt. W2544/1454 700,000 5/15 D. D. & L. A.D.S.S./Forms/C. 2118.

Instructions regarding War Diaries and Intelligence Summaries are contained in F. S. Regs., Part II. and the Staff Manual respectively. Title pages will be prepared in manuscript.

~~INTELLIGENCE SUMMARY.~~

(*Erase heading not required.*)

Place	Date	Hour	Summary of Events and Information	Remarks and references to Appendices
RUBEMPRÉ	17/12/16		Paraded under Section Officers. Recr. Train.	MCS
"	18/12/16		Physical Training and Gun drill under Section Officers. 6 men reported from M.G. Base Depot. 1 N.C.O. + 1 man rejoined from hospital. 1 N.C.O. + 1 man admitted hosp.	MCS
"	19/12/16		Elementary Tactical Training – + P.T.	MCS
"	20/12/16		Training under Section Officers. Capt. W.A. Stanley went on leave. 1 man returned from leave. Recr. Train.	MCS
"	21/12/16		Physical Training under Section Officers. Gun drill. 1 man admitted hospital.	MCS
"	22/12/16		Physical Training under section officers. Drill and Mechanism.	MCS
"	23/12/16		Company paraded for Route March. 1 man proceeded on leave.	MCS
"	24/12/16		Company were fitted with ~~Box~~ Small Box Respirators.	
"	25/12/16		A Football Match was held in the morning and a Concert in the evening. 3 N.C.O's reported from the M.G. Base Depot and 1 man returned from Cold Shoeing Course.	MCS

2353 Wt. W2544/1454 700,000 5/15 D. D. & L. A.D.S.S./Forms/C. 2118.

Summaries are contained in F. S. Regs., Part II. and the Staff Manual respectively. Title pages will be prepared in manuscript.

~~INTELLIGENCE SUMMARY.~~

(Erase heading not required.)

Place	Date	Hour	Summary of Events and Information	Remarks and references to Appendices
RUBEMPRÉ	26/12/16		The Company paraded for a Route March with the Brigade, and marched past the V Army Commander near BEAUQUESNE.	WAS
"			1 N.C.O + 1 man proceeded to M.G. School CAMIERS – 1 N.C.O proceeded to the Vth Army School of Cookery –	
"	27/12/16		All sections carried out Firing on the Range also Physical Training and Mechanism – Recreational Training. 1 N.C.O discharged hospital – 1 N.C.O. + ~~two~~ 1 man admitted hospital – 2/Lt W. HANNAH proceeded on leave. 1 man returned from leave –	WAS.
"	28/12/16		Physical Training – Company drill and Gun drill – Officers Map Reading Course in the evening – Bunking of billets proceeded with – 1 man admitted hospital – Recreational Training	WAS.
"	29/12/16		Company paraded for bombing practice and Stoppage + Drill – Recreational Training – 1 N.C.O. discharged hospital. 1 man returned from leave –	WAS
"	30/12/16		Physical Training – Drill + Mechanism – Recreational Training.	WAS
"	31/12/16		Inspection – Capt W.A. Stanley returned from leave –	

W A Stanley Capt
Commdg 97th M G Coy

2353 Wt. W2534/1454 700,000 5/15 D. D. & L. A.D.S.S./Forms/C. 2118.

Original

97th M.G. Coy.

War Diary for month of January 1917.

Volume XI

[signature] Lieut.
97th Commanding, MACHINE GUN COY.

31-1-17

IX/18

Instructions regarding War Diaries and Intelligence Summaries are contained in F. S. Regs., Part II. and the Staff Manual respectively. Title pages will be prepared in manuscript.

WAR DIARY
or
~~INTELLIGENCE SUMMARY.~~
(Erase heading not required.)

Army Form C. 2118.

Place	Date	Hour	Summary of Events and Information	Remarks and references to Appendices
RUBEMPRÉ	1/1/17		The Company paraded for a Route March – Recreational Tr. in the afternoon – 2/Lt T.W. GREGG & 1 man admitted hospital	[illegible]
"	2/1/17		The Coy. paraded for P.T. and Squad & gun drill and Revolver practice – N.C.O's Map Reading Course –	[illegible]
"	3/1/17		Parades under Section Officers – Recreational Training	[illegible]
"	4/1/17		The Coy. took part in Brigade Training in the attack – 2 men admitted hospital – 2/Lt F.R. CROCOMBE discharged hospital – 2 man proceeded on leave –	[illegible]
"	5/1/17		Coy. paraded for inspection by the C.O. 1 man adm. hosp. 1 man returned off leave –	
COURCELLE	6/1/17		The Coy. proceeded by Bus to COURCELLES – ~~[illegible]~~ Eight guns of the Company relieved Eight guns of 27th M.G.C. in the line opposite SERRE – 2/Lt BROWN & 3 O.R. proceeded to Divisional School. 1 man proceeded on leave – 1 man discharged hospital – 1 man admitted hosp. –	

2353 Wt. W2544/1454 700,000 5/15 D. D. & L. A.D.S.S./Forms/C 2118.

Instructions regarding War Diaries and Intelligence Summaries are contained in F. S. Regs., Part II. and the Staff Manual respectively. Title pages will be prepared in manuscript.

WAR DIARY
or
INTELLIGENCE SUMMARY.

(Erase heading not required.)

Army Form C. 2118.

Place	Date	Hour	Summary of Events and Information	Remarks and references to Appendices
COURCELLES	7/1/17		Coy in the line eight guns in defensive positions and eight in reserve – 2 men discharged hospital – 1 man returned from leave –	
〃	8/1/17		2 men admitted hospital – 1 N.C.O reported for duty from Base – 1 man transferred to Base (under age) –	
〃	9/1/17		Lieut W. HANNAH returned from leave – 1 N.C.O. granted leave	
〃	10/1/17		1 man admitted hospital.	
〃	11/1/17		〃 〃 〃	
〃	12/1/17		1 man returned from leave 1 man admitted hospital	
〃	13/1/17		Lieut N.L.S. POWNALL proceeded on leave – 1 man adm. hosp. 1 man disch. hosp –	
〃	14/1/17		1 N.C.O proceeded to M.G. School CAMIERS – 1 man admitted hospital – The Company was relieved by the 96th M.G. Coy & marched to huts in BUS-EN-ARTOIS –	
〃	15/1/17		2 sections paraded for working party in village and 2	

2353 Wt. W2544/1454 700,000 5/15 D. D. & L. A.D.S.S./Forms/C. 2118.

Instructions regarding War Diaries and Intelligence Summaries are contained in F. S. Regs., Part II. and the Staff Manual respectively. Title pages will be prepared in manuscript.

WAR DIARY
or
INTELLIGENCE SUMMARY.
(Erase heading not required.)

Army Form C. 2118.

Place	Date	Hour	Summary of Events and Information	Remarks and references to Appendices
			sections paraded for ~~[illegible]~~ inspection – Capt W. A. STANLEY proceeded to M.G. School CAMIERS – 1 man discd hosp.	MLA
BUS-EN-ARTOIS	16/1/17		As for 15/1/17 – 2 N.C.Os proceeded to U.K. for the purpose of taking up commissions. 1 N.C.O & 1 man rejoined from M.G. School CAMIERS.	MLA
"	17/1/17		2 section road fatigue – 2 section Training on guns – 1 N.C.O proceeded on leave – 1 man returned from leave –	MLA
"	18/1/17		As for 17/1/17 – two men admitted hospital.	MLA
"	19/1/17		" " " " 2 men admitted hospital – 1 man returned from leave – 1 man proceeded on leave –	
BEAUMONT-HAMEL	20/1/17		The Coy. marched to MAILLY-MAILLET – 9 guns of the 22nd M.G. Coy. were relieved by the Coy in the sector N.E. of BEAUMONT-HAMEL during the afternoon.	
"	21/1/17		4 more guns of 22nd M.G. Coy were relieved by the Coy in the early morning – All positions taken over were situated in reserve area –	

Instructions regarding War Diaries and Intelligence Summaries are contained in F. S. Regs., Part II. and the Staff Manual respectively. Title pages will be prepared in manuscript.

WAR DIARY
or
~~INTELLIGENCE SUMMARY.~~
(Erase heading not required.)

Army Form C. 2118.

Place	Date	Hour	Summary of Events and Information	Remarks and references to Appendices
BEAUMONT HAMEL	22/1/17		1 N.C.O returned from Divisional School – 1 man admitted hospital	MWD –
"	23/1/17		3 guns WEST of WAGON ROAD ~~[illegible]~~ relieved by 14th M.G.C. these guns now being in the 14th Bde area – 1 N.C.O admitted hospital – 1 N.C.O returned from leave –	MWD –
"	24/1/17		2 men proceeded on leave – 1 N.C.O. admitted hospital. 1 man wounded (gassed)	MWD
"	25/1/17		4 guns moved up to advanced posts in FRANKFORT TRENCH LIEUT N.C.C. POWNALL returned from leave –	MWD –
"	26/1/17		2 more guns moved to advanced posts at top of WAGON ROAD – 1 man granted leave –	MWD
"	27/1/17		2 guns moved to advanced post in front of MUCK TRENCH	MWD –
	28/1/17		–	MWD
"	29/1/17		1 man admitted hospital –	MWD
"	30/1/17		1 N.C.O & 2 men admitted to hospital –	
"	31/1/17		2/Lt A.M. HUMBLE. admitted hospital – 1 N.C.O discharged hosp.	MWD –

M W Davidson Lieut
Comdg. 97th M.G. Coy.

2353 Wt. W2544/1454 700,000 5/15 D. D. & L. A.D.S.S./Forms/C. 2118.

97th Machine Gun Coy.

Original War Diary for
February 1917

Volume XII

28th Feby 1917.

[signature]
Lieut
Commanding,
97th MACHINE GUN COY.

Vol 12

Instructions regarding War Diaries and Intelligence Summaries are contained in F. S. Regs., Part II. and the Staff Manual respectively. Title pages will be prepared in manuscript.

WAR DIARY

or

~~INTELLIGENCE SUMMARY.~~

(Erase heading not required.)

Army Form C. 2118.

Place	Date	Hour	Summary of Events and Information	Remarks and references to Appendices
BEAMONT-HAMEL	1/2/17		Company in the line – 8 guns in advanced posts – 1 Btty. M.M. Guns and Six guns of 96th M.G. Coy. attached –	[illegible]
"	2/2/17		Coy. in line – 1 man admitted hospital –	[illegible]
"	3/2/17		Six more guns pushed forward to advanced posts on the right of Bde. Sector, to strengthen junction of 97th Bde and 188th Bde for the attack by the 63rd Div. 1 N.C.O returned from leave –	[illegible]
"	4/2/17		As for 3/2/17 – Capt W. A. STANLEY returned from M.G. School 2/Lt L.S.B. BROWN returned from Divisional School 2/Lt A.M. HUMBLE returned from Hospital – Coy in the line 1 man returned from leave – " "	[illegible]
"	5/2/17		2 men rejoined from hospital – " "	[illegible]
"	6/2/17		1 man admitted hospital – " "	[illegible]
"	7/2/17		2 men proceeded to M.G. School – 1 man proceeded to shoeing course ABBEVILLE. 1 N.C.O. proceeded to U.K. on admission to Cadet School 2 men wounded –	

2353 Wt. W2544/1454 700,000 5/15 D. D. & L. A.D.S.S./Forms/C. 2118.

Instructions regarding War Diaries and Intelligence Summaries are contained in F. S. Regs., Part II. and the Staff Manual respectively. Title pages will be prepared in manuscript.

WAR DIARY
or
INTELLIGENCE SUMMARY.
(Erase heading not required.)

Army Form C. 2118.

Place	Date	Hour	Summary of Events and Information	Remarks and references to Appendices
BEAUMONT HAMEL			Coy in the line	
	8/2/17		1 man returned from leave – 1 man went on leave	MWS
"	9/2/17		2 men rejoined from hospital – 3 men admitted hospital.	
			1 man returned from leave – "	MWS
"	10/2/17		2/Lt RHODES and 4 men reported from M.G. BASE DEPOT	
			The Coy. assisted 97th Inf. Bde in its attack on TEN TREE ALLEY – Attached Appendix gives Action of Company –	MWS
			Casualties – Killed Two – Died of wounds Two – Wounded Four.	
"	11/2/17		1 man admitted hospital –	
"	12/2/17		Guns in forward posts who had taken part in the operation of the 10th/11th were relieved by 1st M.M.G Btty and by guns of 96th M.G. Coy –	MWS
"	13/2/17		97th Inf. Bde was relieved by 185th Bde 62nd Div. The Coy. remained in the line and were attached to 185th Inf. Bde –	
			1 N.C.O 2 men discharged hospital –	MWS.
"	14/2/17		2/Lt N. PICKTHALL admitted hospital – 2 men adm. Hosp.	MWS

2353 Wt. W2544/1454 700,000 5/15 D. D. & L. A.D.S.S./Forms/C. 2118.

Instructions regarding War Diaries and Intelligence Summaries are contained in F. S. Regs., Part II. and the Staff Manual respectively. Title pages will be prepared in manuscript.

WAR DIARY
or
INTELLIGENCE SUMMARY.
(Erase heading not required.)

Army Form C. 2118.

Place	Date	Hour	Summary of Events and Information	Remarks and references to Appendices
BEAUMONT-HAMEL	15/2/17		1st M.M.G. Bty & guns of 98th M.G. Coy. relieved by guns of 97th M.G. Coy—	[illegible]
"	16/2/17		2 men admitted Hospital— 15 men reported from M.G. Base Depot—	[illegible]
"	17/2/17		2 men admitted hospital— 1 man discharged from hospital	[illegible]
ARPONVILLE	18/2/17		The Coy. were relieved during night 17/18th by guns of 22nd M.G. Coy and 91st M.G. Coy. (7th Division)— The Coy. marched to Billets in HARPONVILLE— 2 men discharged from Hospital—	[illegible]
ADENCOURT	19/2/17		The Coy. marched to VADENCOURT— 5 men adm. hospital	[illegible]
"	20/2/17		Coy. inspected by C.O. 2 men rejoined from hospital	[illegible]
T. ACHEUL	21/2/17		The Coy. marched to ST. ACHEUL (AMIENS)—	
UBERCOURT	22/2/17		The Coy. marched to AUBERCOURT—	
"	23/2/17		Guns and Equipment overhauled and checked— 2/Lt A. SMITH and 26 men reported from M.G. Base Depot. 1 man admitted hospital— 1 man discharged hospital	[illegible]

2353 Wt. W2544/1454 700,000 5/15 D. D. & L. A.D.S.S./Forms/C. 2118.

Instructions regarding War Diaries and Intelligence Summaries are contained in F. S. Regs., Part II. and the Staff Manual respectively. Title pages will be prepared in manuscript.

WAR DIARY
or
INTELLIGENCE SUMMARY.
(Erase heading not required.)

Army Form C. 2118.

Place	Date	Hour	Summary of Events and Information	Remarks and references to Appendices
AUBERCOURT	24/2/17		Company paraded for training under Section Officers – 1 man reported for duty from 2nd K.O.Y.L.I.	[initials]
BEAUCOURT			The Coy. marched to billets in BEAUCOURT	
	25/2/17		2/Lt T RHODES and 2 men proceeded to M.G. School, CAMIERS. 1 N.C.O proceeded to join 94th M.G. Coy. on appointment as C.S.M.	[initials]
"	26/2/17		Training under Section Officers – Recreational Training in the afternoon. 1 man returned from leave – 2 men reported from 16th H.L.I. 2 men from 11th BORDER REGT 1 man from 2nd K.O.Y.L.I. 2 men from 17th H.L.I. 1 N.C.O & 2 men admitted hospital – Two men rejoined from M.G. School –	[initials]
"	27/2/17		Training under Sect. Officers – Recr. Train in afternoon 2 men admitted hospital –	
"	28.2.17		Inspection by Divisional Commander in morning. Recreational training in afternoon	

W. A. Stanley major
97th Machine Gun Coy

2353 Wt. W2544/1454 700,000 5/15 D. D. & L. A.D.S.S./Forms/C. 2118.

Army Form C. 2118.

WAR DIARY

or

~~INTELLIGENCE SUMMARY.~~

(Erase heading not required.)

Instructions regarding War Diaries and Intelligence Summaries are contained in F. S. Regs., Part II. and the Staff Manual respectively. Title pages will be prepared in manuscript.

Place	Date	Hour	Summary of Events and Information	Remarks and references to Appendices
			APPENDIX to Entry dated 10/2/17 —	
			ACTION of 97th M.G. Coy. during attack on TENTREE ALLEY — REF. SHEETS — REDAN and PENDANT COPSE 1:5000	
			ACTION of No 1 Section —	
			On the night of the 10th/11th Feb. 4 guns of No 2 Section and 2 guns of No 1 Section (2/Lt PICKTHALL) under 2/Lt F.R. CROCOMBE left Company H.Q ~~at~~ (BEAMONT-HAMEL) at 5.30 p.m. — at 7.10 p.m. the guns were in position & all laid on their respective targets —	
			2 guns at PLUM POST	
			" " " POLL'S PERCH.	
			" " " GUN POST.	
			The targets consisted of GLORY LANE and two enemy M. Guns — The guns were also [laid?] to form a barrage in front of the field gun barrage —	
			At Zero hour (8.30 p.m.) the guns opened fire on the allotted targets — At 8.45 pm it was reported	

Army Form C. 2118.

Instructions regarding War Diaries and Intelligence Summaries are contained in F. S. Regs., Part II. and the Staff Manual respectively. Title pages will be prepared in manuscript.

WAR DIARY
or
INTELLIGENCE SUMMARY.
(Erase heading not required.)

Place	Date	Hour	Summary of Events and Information	Remarks and references to Appendices
			that ~~the~~ one gun at GUN POST was out of action – the other gun at GUN POST immediately engaged both targets –	
			At 9.10 p.m. the 11th BORDER REGT were seen advancing over the ridge in R1a to the objective and the guns were ordered to cease fire to avoid hitting our own troops –	
			At 10.30 p.m. 2/Lt CROCOMBE went forward to R1a 5 5 in GLORY LANE and reported to O.C. 11th BORDER REGT. who ordered two guns to go forward to protect the left flank of the battalion which was exposed – One gun was placed near a burning dugout in the captured trench and another about 100 yds west of it.	
			At about 3.30 a.m. on the 11th the enemy under cover of the smoke from the burning dugout started to bomb along the trench – One gun was rushed and the sergeant i/c. killed and one man wounded.	
			2/Lt CROCOMBE sent 2/Lt PICKTHALL back to PLUM POST for another	

2353 Wt. W2544/1454 700,000 5/15 D. D. & L. A.D.S.S./Forms/C. 2118.

Instructions regarding War Diaries and Intelligence Summaries are contained in F. S. Regs., Part II. and the Staff Manual respectively. Title pages will be prepared in manuscript.

WAR DIARY
or
INTELLIGENCE SUMMARY.
(Erase heading not required.)

Army Form C. 2118.

Place	Date	Hour	Summary of Events and Information	Remarks and references to Appendices
			gun which arrived at about 4.0 a.m. and came into action on the raided trench. At about 4.15 a.m. the bombing slackened and by 5.0 a.m. the counter attack had ceased. Two more men were wounded. When it became light an enemy gun with ammunition was found and mounted and was used with effect on enemy seen moving on white cliff east of captured position. About this time 2/Lt CROCOMBE and SERGT LEWIS went to look for SERGT SAUNDERS' whose gun had been raided. They found his body but no trace of the gun. This however had been found and brought in by LT SIMCOCK. 97th T.M. 13th. When looking for the gun SERGT LEWIS captured a prisoner. The total number of rounds fired during the barrage was 13000 and during the counter attack 1750, exclusive of those fired from the captured enemy gun.	

2353 Wt. W2544/1454 700,000 5/15 D. D. & L. A.D.S.S./Forms/C. 2118.

Instructions regarding War Diaries and Intelligence Summaries are contained in F. S. Regs., Part II. and the Staff Manual respectively. Title pages will be prepared in manuscript.

WAR DIARY
or
INTELLIGENCE SUMMARY.
(Erase heading not required.)

Army Form C. 2118.

Place	Date	Hour	Summary of Events and Information	Remarks and references to Appendices
			Action of No. 3 Section under Lt. HANNAH.	
			No 3. Section relieved 4 guns of the 1st M.M.G. Bty. at 6.30 p.m. on 10/2/17 and took up positions for the attack, in support of the 2nd K.O.Y.L.I. as follows:	
			2 guns GOUGH POST (No 1 & 2)	
			1 — FRANKFORT POST (No 3)	
			1 — BANTAMS NEST (No 4)	
			At 12 Midnight O.C. 2nd K.O.Y.L.I. sent forward 2 guns (No 3 & 4) to assist the infantry in holding the ground they had reported as gained. Communication with the Battns on the flanks had been temporarily lost so No 4 gun was placed at K36d. 4.9. to cover C. Coy. front, while consolidating, and to protect their left Flank. An Enemy post still held out at K631c 5.3. and its M.G. was troubling our infantry on the right. No 3 gun was therefore placed at K36d 9.3. covering this post and the valley south of LAGER VALLEY.	

2353 Wt. W2544/1454 700,000 5/15 D. D. & L. A.D.S.S./Forms/C. 2118.

Instructions regarding War Diaries and Intelligence Summaries are contained in F. S. Regs., Part II. and the Staff Manual respectively. Title pages will be prepared in manuscript.

WAR DIARY
or
INTELLIGENCE SUMMARY.
(Erase heading not required.)

Army Form C. 2118.

Place	Date	Hour	Summary of Events and Information	Remarks and references to Appendices
			97th M.G. Coy	
			At 9 a.m. on 11th Feb. 2/Lt BROWN and 3 O.R. 2nd K.O.Y.L.I. discovered a dugout in LAGER ALLEY that the mopping up parties had not cleared – 27 prisoners were taken and handed over to an Escort from 2nd K.O.Y.L.I.	
			Meanwhile the 2 teams at GOUGH POST moved forward and occupied the position vacated by Nos 3 & 4 teams –	
			At 11 p.m. on 11th No 3 team provided covering fire to a bombing attack carried out by A Coy. 2nd K.O.Y.L.I. against enemy post in the trees in TENTREE ALLEY. Several enemy casualties were reported as the result of this fire –	
			As the bombing attack failed it was decided to withdraw this gun from the advanced post to LAGER ALLEY, a Lewis gun being substituted –	
			On the night of the twelfth the section was relieved by 1st M.M.G. Btty. During the operation the section lost two men died of wounds –	

2353 Wt. W2544/1454 700,000 5/15 D. D. & L. A.D.S.S./Forms/C. 2118.

Instructions regarding War Diaries and Intelligence Summaries are contained in F. S. Regs., Part II. and the Staff Manual respectively. Title pages will be prepared in manuscript.

WAR DIARY
or
INTELLIGENCE SUMMARY.
(Erase heading not required.)

Army Form C. 2118.

Place	Date	Hour	Summary of Events and Information	Remarks and references to Appendices
			ACTION of No 4 section – On the night 10th/11th 4 guns No 4 section and two guns No 1 section the whole under Lt HUMBLE were distributed as follows: 2 guns (No 4 sect) AXLE POST – (under LT. HUMBLE) – " " " " " in reserve at Coy. H. Q. " " (No 1 sect) " " " WALKER QUARRY (under 2/Lt RHODES) O.C. 16th Northumberland Fusiliers expected a counter attack to come from WHITE TRENCH and wished fire to be brought to bear on this trench – This was done from AXLE POST – Fire was opened at about 8.30 p.m. and was carried on during the night – W. W. Stanley major Commdg 97th Machine Gun Coy.	

Headquarters
97th Inf Bde

No. 97 MACHINE GUN COMPANY.
No. 545
Date 31-3-17.

Herewith original War Diary for March 1917.

W A Stanley Major
Commanding,
97th MACHINE GUN COY.

31-3-17.

H.Q. 97TH INFANTRY BDE.
No. 891
Date 31/3/17

9th Machine Gun Coy

Original War Diary for

Month of March 1917.

Volume XIII

W.A. Stanley Major

Commanding 9th M.G. Coy.

Vol 13

Army Form C. 2118.

Instructions regarding War Diaries and Intelligence Summaries are contained in F. S. Regs., Part II. and the Staff Manual respectively. Title pages will be prepared in manuscript.

WAR DIARY
or
~~INTELLIGENCE SUMMARY.~~
(Erase heading not required.)

Place	Date	Hour	Summary of Events and Information	Remarks and references to Appendices
BEAUCOURT EN-SANTERRE	1/3/17		Coy. paraded for Training under section officers. Recreational Training in the afternoon. 1 man discharged from hospital 1 man admitted to hospital.	[illegible]
"	2/3/17		Training under Section Officers. Recreational Training. 2 men discharged from hospital. 1 N.C.O & 1 man admitted to hospital.	[illegible]
ROUVROY	3/3/17		The Coy. relieved 16 guns of the 14th M.G. Coy. in the ROUVROY Sector. in the line. 1 man accidentally wounded. 1 man proceeded on leave.	[illegible]
"	4/3/17		The Coy. in the line. Indirect Fire carried out night and day.	[illegible]
"	5/3/17		Coy. in the line. Indirect Fire carried out night & day.	[illegible]
"	6/3/17		Coy. in the line. " " " " " " LT. A. M. HUMBLE proceeded to BASE DEPOT for Dental Treatment 1 man discharged from hospital.	[illegible]

A5834 Wt. W4973 M687 750,000 8/16 D. D. & L. Ltd. Forms/C.2118/13.

Instructions regarding War Diaries and Intelligence Summaries are contained in F. S. Regs., Part II. and the Staff Manual respectively. Title pages will be prepared in manuscript.

WAR DIARY
or
~~INTELLIGENCE SUMMARY.~~
(Erase heading not required.)

Army Form C. 2118.

Place	Date	Hour	Summary of Events and Information	Remarks and references to Appendices
ROUVROY	7/3/17		Coy. in the line – Indirect fire carried out intermittently – 1 N.C.O. proceeded to M.G. Corps Base Depot – 1 man admitted to hospital –	[illegible]
"	8/3/17		Coy. in the line – Indirect fire carried out – 2 men admitted to hospital –	[illegible]
"	9/3/17		Coy. in the line – 1 N.C.O. and 1 man discharged from hospital –	[illegible]
"	10/3/17		Coy. in the line – 4 guns on the left of Bde. Sector were relieved by 1 section of 104th M.G. Coy. These four guns then relieved 1 section of 96th M.G. Coy on the right of Bde. Sector –	[illegible]
"	11/3/17		Coy. in the line – Indirect fire carried out intermittently	

A5834 Wt. W4973 M687 750,000 8/16 D. D. & L. Ltd. Forms/C.2118/13.

Instructions regarding War Diaries and Intelligence Summaries are contained in F. S. Regs., Part II. and the Staff Manual respectively. Title pages will be prepared in manuscript.

WAR DIARY
or
INTELLIGENCE SUMMARY.
(Erase heading not required.)

Army Form C. 2118.

Place	Date	Hour	Summary of Events and Information	Remarks and references to Appendices
ROUVROY	12/3/17		Coy. in the line – at 6.15 p.m. all guns opened fire on FOUQUESCOURT for three minutes for Dummy Raid – Indirect fire carried out – 1 N.C.O. and one man admitted hospital –	[illegible]
"	13/3/17		Coy. in the line – Indirect fire carried out night and day. 1 man admitted to hospital – 1 man discharged from hospital – 1 man wounded and remained at duty –	[illegible]
"	14/3/17		Coy. in the line – Indirect fire carried out – 1 man admitted to hospital –	[illegible]
"	15/3/17		The Coy. was relieved in the line by 14th M.G. Coy. and proceeded to billets in BEAUCOURT – 1 man discharged from hospital –	[illegible]

A5834 Wt. W4973 M687 750,000 8/16 D. D. & L. Ltd. Forms/C.2118/13.

Army Form C. 2118.

Instructions regarding War Diaries and Intelligence Summaries are contained in F. S. Regs., Part II. and the Staff Manual respectively. Title pages will be prepared in manuscript.

WAR DIARY
or
~~INTELLIGENCE SUMMARY.~~

(Erase heading not required.)

Place	Date	Hour	Summary of Events and Information	Remarks and references to Appendices
MEZIERES	16/3/17		The Coy. moved to billets in MEZIERES – 2 men discharged from hospital – 1 man admitted to hospital –	[illegible]
BEAUFORT WOOD	17/3/17		The Coy. moved to Huts in BEAUFORT WOOD –	[illegible]
LA CHAVATTE	18/3/17		" " " to ROUVROY and in evening advanced to LA CHAVATTE – 1 man returned from leave – 1 man discharged from hospital – 1 N.C.O. and 1 man proceeded to M.G. School Camiers – 1 N.C.O rejoined from M.G. School –	[illegible]
HERLY	19/3/17		Coy. moved to HERLY – 2/Lt F.R. CROCOMBE proceeded to England. Auth. A.G. a/22707/5 dated 14/3/17 – 1 man granted leave –	[illegible]
NESLE	20/3/17		Coy. moved to NESLE –	[illegible]
"	21/3/17.		The Coy. furnished working parties on roads etc.	

A5834 Wt. W4973 M687 750,000 8/16 D. D. & L. Ltd. Forms/C.2118/13.

Instructions regarding War Diaries and Intelligence Summaries are contained in F. S. Regs., Part II. and the Staff Manual respectively. Title pages will be prepared in manuscript.

WAR DIARY
or
INTELLIGENCE SUMMARY.
(Erase heading not required.)

Army Form C. 2118.

Place	Date	Hour	Summary of Events and Information	Remarks and references to Appendices
NESLE.	22/3/17.		Coy. furnished working parties. Guns cleaned & limbers packed. 2/Lt N. PICKTHALL admitted to hospital. 2/Lt T. RHODES & 1 man returned from M.G. School CAMIERS.	[illegible]
"	23/3/17		Coy. furnished working parties. LT A.M. HUMBLE rejoined from BASE DEPOT ETAPLES. 1 man admitted to hospital.	[illegible]
"	24/3/17		Coy. furnished working parties.	
"	25/3/17		Coy. furnished working parties and attended Church parade	[illegible]
"	26/3/17		" " " " — 1 man rejoined from hospital.	[illegible]
"	27/3/17		Coy. furnished working parties. 1 man admitted hospital.	[illegible]

Army Form C. 2118.

Instructions regarding War Diaries and Intelligence Summaries are contained in F. S. Regs., Part II. and the Staff Manual respectively. Title pages will be prepared in manuscript.

WAR DIARY

or

~~INTELLIGENCE SUMMARY.~~

(Erase heading not required.)

Place	Date	Hour	Summary of Events and Information	Remarks and references to Appendices
FORESTE.	28/3/17		The ~~A~~ company moved to the line – Eight guns took up positions ~~to the~~ in the outpost line to the N. + E. of ETREILLERS – The remaining eight guns remained in reserve at FORESTE –	[illegible]
FORESTE.	29/3/17.		The Coy. in the line – Parties of the enemy fired on and dispersed –	[illegible]
"	30/3/17.		The Coy. in the line –	[illegible]
"	31/3/17.		The Coy. in the line –	[illegible]

W A [illegible] Major
Commdg 97th M G Coy

A5834 Wt. W4973 M687 750,000 8/16 D. D. & L. Ltd. Forms/C.2118/13.

Confidential

97th M.G. Coy

Original War Diary
for month of
April 1917.

Volume XIII

W.C. Davidson
Lieut
Commanding,
97th MACHINE GUN COY.

30-4-17.

Vol 14

WAR DIARY
or
~~INTELLIGENCE~~ SUMMARY.
(*Erase heading not required.*)

Army Form C. 2118.

Instructions regarding War Diaries and Intelligence Summaries are contained in F. S. Regs., Part II. and the Staff Manual respectively. Title pages will be prepared in manuscript.

Place	Date	Hour	Summary of Events and Information	Remarks and references to Appendices
SAVY	1.4.17		The 97th Inf Bde attacked SAVY at 5 am on Apl 1st. 97th Machine Gun Coy supported the attack by putting up an enfilade barrage. A considerable number of casualties were inflicted on the enemy by this M G Barrage. 8 guns took up positions on the ETREILLERS - SAVY Road at about X28.c5.5 & fired on the S. outskirts of SAVY during the first stages of the attack lifting to the N outskirts as the attack proceeded. These 8 guns remained in X28c5.5 position throughout the day	Map Ref 62C $\frac{1}{40,000}$
		4.15am	The 2 other sections (Nos 2 & 4) took up positions in front of ROUPY in a disused trench post & opened fire at Zero (5 am) on roads & tracks around SAVY fire was kept up till 5.15 am when the sections prepared to move forward.	W.A.E.
		5.25am	These 8 guns moved across in extended order to the captured village entering the village by the road at X29d7.0, the barrier at the cross roads was still in position & an enemy machine gun opened fire on the sections from the ruins of the village. The teams took cover in a ditch & so only sustained one slight casualty. The M.G. very soon withdrew. 4 guns were put into position to support the ~~left~~ right Bn. The enemy was still holding a strong point on the left, so the other 4 gun teams used their rifles & assisted the infantry, the strong point was cleared at 7am & 4 guns were then put in position on the Railway embankment at X30a covering the whole of the N of SAVY 2 men admitted to Hospital.	
	2.4.17		Nos 1 & 3 sections moved forward to Quarry N.E. of ROUPY to support the 16th HLI who were forming a defensive flank for the French attack on DALLON, 4 guns	W.A.E.

A5834 Wt. W4973 M687 750,000 8/16 D. D. & L. Ltd. Forms/C.2118/13.

Instructions regarding War Diaries and Intelligence Summaries are contained in F. S. Regs., Part II. and the Staff Manual respectively. Title pages will be prepared in manuscript.

WAR DIARY
or
~~INTELLIGENCE SUMMARY.~~
(Erase heading not required.)

Army Form C. 2118.

2

Place	Date	Hour	Summary of Events and Information	Remarks and references to Appendices
			went forward & took up positions in the posts the other 4 guns remained in support at the Quarry which was heavily shelled throughout the day &	
	2.4.17		night.	
			Nos 2 & 4 sections remained in position at SAVY.	WAE
			9 men wounded 8 men admitted hospital 2nd Lt FR CROCOMBE struck off the strength on being accepted for the Indian Army	
	3.4.17		2 sections withdrawn to ETREILLERS & 2 to bivouacs in SAVY for a rest 1 O.R. admitted hospital ~~1 man to Base~~ [illegible] ~~4 O.R. wounded 3 O.R. admitted hospital~~	WAE
	4.4.17		Coy distributed as above	
	5.4.17		" " " "	
	6.4.17		Relieved 14th MG Coy in the line HOLNON - FRANCILLY - SELENCY in the evening. 2 OR wounded	
	7.4.17		Company distributed as above. Guns fired day & night on various targets. 2nd Lieut M.A. CRAMSHAW & 7 O.R. reinforcements from Base. 2 O.R. wounded.	
	8.4.17		as the 7th	
	9.4.17		" " " 2 o.r. admitted hospital.	WAE
	10.4.17		" " " 1 o.r. wounded	
	11.4.17		" " " 3 o.r. hospital 10 o.r. reinforcements from Base	
	12.4.17		" " "	
	13.4.17		" " "	
	14.4.17		97th Infantry Bde attacked ~~[illegible]~~ FAYET at 4.30 a.m. 97 MG Coy & 219 MG Coy (under orders from O.C. 97 MG Coy) supported the attack as follows.	

A5834 Wt. W4973 M687 750,000 8/16 D. D. & L. Ltd. Forms/C.2118/13.

Instructions regarding War Diaries and Intelligence Summaries are contained in F. S. Regs., Part II. and the Staff Manual respectively. Title pages will be prepared in manuscript.

WAR DIARY
or
INTELLIGENCE SUMMARY.
(Erase heading not required.)

Army Form C. 2118.

3

Place	Date	Hour	Summary of Events and Information	Remarks and references to Appendices
	14.4.17		4 sections took up positions & dug themselves in in M33. 3 section did the same just S of the BOIS de ROSES, (a covering party being supplied by the infantry to cover the latter sections whilst digging in as no infantry were near this position) 1 section was held in reserve. At Zero all guns opened fire on roads tracks & positions thought to be used or occupied by the enemy. This fire was continued for 1 hr 15 m the barrage lifting as the infantry advanced. The village of FAYET was captured. At about 6 am. 5 sections went forward & took up defensive positions to support the infantry. Of these 5 sections 2½ were from 97 Coy & 2½ from 219 Coy. (3 section remained in M33) 6 guns of 97 Coy were detailed to support the right Bn (16th H.L.I.) these guns were placed on the S of FAYET & as no counter attack was launched by the enemy, they did not fire. 4 guns were detailed to support the left Bn (2nd KOYLI). These guns took up positions in the sunken road on the N of FAYET, facing the Twin copses, several parties of the enemy were seen & fired on. At 1 pm the 11th Border Regt attacked the TWIN COPSES & these guns were employed to form a moving barrage, 6 guns in M33 also fired at & around the Twin copses, a number of the enemy were seen to be killed by this fire & after the copses had been taken a number of dead	[illegible initials]

A5834 Wt. W4973/M687 750,000 8/16 D. D. & L. Ltd. Forms/C.2118/13.

Instructions regarding War Diaries and Intelligence Summaries are contained in F. S. Regs., Part II. and the Staff Manual respectively. Title pages will be prepared in manuscript.

WAR DIARY
or
INTELLIGENCE SUMMARY.
(Erase heading not required.)

Army Form C. 2118.

4

Place	Date	Hour	Summary of Events and Information	Remarks and references to Appendices
	14.4.17		were found. A number of dead were also found in FAYET. The infantry report that an enemy M.G. was heard to fire about 20 rounds as they were advancing on FAYET, when fire was suddenly ceased, this gun was found behind the hedge on the S.W. of FAYET, the gunner had been killed by M.G. fire, 4 bullet holes were in the gun, several bullet marks on the tripod the trees around were all chipped by M.G. fire	W.A.E.
			Casualties 2nd Lieut A SMITH wounded	
	15.4.17		The coy was relieved at 8 pm by 96 M.G. Coy withdrew to FORESTE to Divl reserve 3 OR admitted hospital	W.A.E.
FORESTE	16.4.17		Cleaning up generally	W.A.E.
"	17.4.17		Section training	W.A.E.
"	18.4.17		" " 1 OR. admitted 2 OR. discharged hospital	W.A.E.
	19.4.17		Company proceeded to Corps reserve at HOMBLEUX 9 OR. reinforcements from base	W.A.E.
HOMBLEUX	20.4.17 to 23.4.17		Training 20th 1 OR discharged hospital 21 1 OR admitted 2 OR. discharged hospital 22. 2nd Lieut O.V. BARKER + 2 OR. reported from base 24 2 OR discharged hospital	W.A.E.
	24.4.17		Company marched to billets in OFFOY	W.A.E.

A5834 Wt. W4973/M687 750,000 8/16 D. D. & L. Ltd. Forms/C.2118/13.

Instructions regarding War Diaries and Intelligence Summaries are contained in F. S. Regs., Part II. and the Staff Manual respectively. Title pages will be prepared in manuscript.

WAR DIARY
or
INTELLIGENCE SUMMARY.
(Erase heading not required.)

Army Form C. 2118.

5

Place	Date	Hour	Summary of Events and Information	Remarks and references to Appendices
OFFOY	25	25.4.17	Company Training. Transport inspected by Brigadier. 3 OR admitted hospital	
"	26.4.17		" " 1 OR reported from base	
"	27.4.17		" "	
"			Major N.A. Stanley proceeded to England on leave	
"	28.4.17		Company Training	
"			Lieut Davidson VC returned from leave 1 OR discharged from hospital; 1 OR admitted hospital. 1 OR proceeded to base on instructional course	
	29.4.17		Church Parade. 2 OR admitted hospital. 1 OR returned from course	
	30.4.17		Brigade inspected by Divisional General	

[signature] Lieut
Comdg 97th M.G. Coy

A5834 Wt. W4973 M687 750,000 8/16 D. D. & L. Ltd. Forms/C.2118/13.

97th M.G. Coy.

Original War Diary
for May 1917

Volume XV

Vol 15

31.5.17.

W. A. Stanley. Major
COMMANDING
97TH MACHINE GUN COMPANY

Instructions regarding War Diaries and Intelligence Summaries are contained in F. S. Regs., Part II. and the Staff Manual respectively. Title pages will be prepared in manuscript.

WAR DIARY
or
~~INTELLIGENCE SUMMARY.~~
(Erase heading not required.)

Army Form C. 2118.

Place	Date	Hour	Summary of Events and Information	Remarks and references to Appendices
May 1st — May 14th			The Company was Training at OFFOY_	
May 18th — May 29th			The Company was Training at THEZY_	
May 30th			The Company moved to VILLERS - BRETONNEUX_	
" 31st			Coy at VILLERS-BRETONNEUX	
			During the month 2 N.C.Os and 10 men were evacuated to C.C.S. and were struck off the Strength	
			2/Lt. J.F. BURNS reported from M.G. Base Depot and was taken on the Strength_	
			1 N.C.O was struck off the strength on appointment to 192nd M.G. Coy as C.S.M.	
			1 N.C.O was taken on strength on appointment as C.Q.M.S.	[initials]

W.W. Stark[?] Major.
COMMANDING
[stamp: ... COMPANY]

Original

War Deary for month of June

VOL. XI

97 M G Coy
Oct 16

Army Form C. 2118.

Instructions regarding War Diaries and Intelligence Summaries are contained in F. S. Regs., Part II. and the Staff Manual respectively. Title pages will be prepared in manuscript.

WAR DIARY
or
~~INTELLIGENCE SUMMARY.~~

(*Erase heading not required.*)

Place	Date	Hour	Summary of Events and Information	Remarks and references to Appendices
DOULIEU AREA.	1·6·17 to 13·6·17		The Company was training in the DOULIEU AREA.	[illegible]
DUNKERQUE AREA	14·6·17 –16·6·17		The Company moved by march-route and by Bus to the S. POL-SUR-MER, DUNKERQUE.	[illegible]
COXYDE AREA.	18·6·17		The Company moved by Train to the COXYDE AREA.	[illegible]
	19·6·17 to 26·6·17		The Company in Divisional Reserve, Training, in the COXYDE AREA.	[illegible]
NIEUPORT	27·6·17		On the night 26th/27th 6.17. the Company relieved the 14th COY M.G.C. in the Left Subsector, Divisional Front, NIEUPORT Sector.	[illegible]
NIEUPORT.	27·6·17 to 30·6·17		Company in the line, NIEUPORT Sector. Nothing special to report, average 8000, rounds fired per night on enemy support lines & roads.	[illegible]

[signature] Capt.
Comdg 94th M.G. Coy

Army Form C. 2118.

Instructions regarding War Diaries and Intelligence Summaries are contained in F. S. Regs., Part II. and the Staff Manual respectively. Title pages will be prepared in manuscript.

WAR DIARY
or
~~INTELLIGENCE SUMMARY.~~

(*Erase heading not required.*)

Place	Date	Hour	Summary of Events and Information	Remarks and references to Appendices
			During the Month:	
			MAJOR W. A. STANLEY apptd. Divisional M.G.O 32nd Div. & Struck off Strength	(25.6.17)
			CAPT. I. A. LEESON assumed command of the Coy. from 219th Coy M.G.C.	(25.6.17)
			Three N.C.O's and Four men reported from M.G.C. Base Depot and were taken on the Strength.	
			Two men were evacuated to C.C.S and struck off strength	
			One man was killed in Action.	
			One man died of wounds.	
			One man wounded.	
			Ian A. Leeson Capt. Comdg 94th Infy Coy.	

A5834 Wt. W4973 M687 750,000 8/16 D. D. & L. Ltd. Forms/C.2118/13.

97th M. G. Coy

32nd Divn

ORIGINAL.

Vol 17

WAR DIARY

FOR

JULY 1917

VOLUME XII

Instructions regarding War Diaries and Intelligence Summaries are contained in F. S. Regs., Part II. and the Staff Manual respectively. Title pages will be prepared in manuscript.

WAR DIARY

or

~~INTELLIGENCE SUMMARY.~~

(Erase heading not required.)

Army Form C. 2118.

Place	Date	Hour	Summary of Events and Information	Remarks and references to Appendices
			From the 1st July to the 13th July the Company was in the line in the LOMBARTZYDE Sector at NIEUPORT.	
			7 guns were in the second line, 4 in the 3rd line and 5 in Reserve. Indirect overhead fire was carried out every night from the Reserve Positions.	
			During the attack by the enemy on the 10th July the Coy. lost 9 guns. Of these 3 were missing, 2 buried and unable to be salved, and 4 destroyed.	
			70 Casualties were incurred, including Capt. I.A. LEESON and 2/Lt I.F. BURNS killed and 2/Lt T. RHODES wounded.	
			The Coy was relieved by the 14th Coy M.G.C. on the night 13th/14th inst.	
			From the 15th to 19th the Coy was at COXYDE.	
			During this time eight guns took up Anti-aircraft	

A5834 Wt. W4973/M687 750,000 8/16 D. D. & L. Ltd. Forms/C.2118/13.

Instructions regarding War Diaries and Intelligence Summaries are contained in F. S. Regs., Part II. and the Staff Manual respectively. Title pages will be prepared in manuscript.

WAR DIARY
or
INTELLIGENCE SUMMARY.
(Erase heading not required.)

Army Form C. 2118.

Place	Date	Hour	Summary of Events and Information	Remarks and references to Appendices
			position for the defence of Dunkirk.	
			From the 20th to the 31st the remaining Eight guns were training at BRAY-DUNE PLAGE.	
			On the 31st the A.A. guns were relieved by the 49th Division and the Coy marched to COXYDE.	
			During the month, besides the Officers mentioned above the following were struck off the strength.	
			1 W.O. 4 N.C.O's. 60 men.	
			Capt. F.W. Gordon, (29/7/17) Lieut W.E. HOWARD and 2/LT H.E. GARSIN (14/7/17) reported from Base Depot and taken on strength.	
			4 N.C.O's, 51 men ~~to~~ reported from Base Depot and taken on strength.	
			20 men attached from Infantry.	
			[illegible] Lieut for Capt. Commdg 97th Coy M.G.C.	

CONFIDENTIAL

Vol 18

97th M. G. Coy.

WAR DIARY

FOR

AUGUST 1917.

VOLUME XIII

Army Form C. 2118.

Instructions regarding War Diaries and Intelligence Summaries are contained in F. S. Regs., Part II. and the Staff Manual respectively. Title pages will be prepared in manuscript.

WAR DIARY
or
~~INTELLIGENCE SUMMARY.~~
(Erase heading not required.)

Place	Date	Hour	Summary of Events and Information	Remarks and references to Appendices
COXYDE	1/8/17 – 14/8/17		The Company was in Divisional Reserve	[illegible]
BRAY-DUNES	15/8/17 – 17/8/17		The Company was in Corps Reserve, Training –	[illegible]
GHYVELDE	18/8/17 – 27/8/17			
S. GEORGES SECTOR –	28/8/17 – 31/8/17		On the night 28th/29th the Company relieved the 98th Coy M.G.C. in the line in the S. GEORGES SECTOR – with 12 guns in the line – The remaining Four guns went into the line on the night 30th/31st.	[illegible]

A5834 Wt. W4973/M687 750,000 8/16 D. D. & L. Ltd. Forms/C.2118/13.

Army Form C. 2118.

Instructions regarding War Diaries and Intelligence Summaries are contained in F. S. Regs., Part II. and the Staff Manual respectively. Title pages will be prepared in manuscript.

WAR DIARY
or
~~INTELLIGENCE SUMMARY.~~
(Erase heading not required.)

Place	Date	Hour	Summary of Events and Information	Remarks and references to Appendices
			During the Month:	
			2/Lt. M. A. CRAWSHAW M.C. was struck off the strength	
			5 men were struck off the strength.	[illegible]
			2 N.C.O's and 5 men were taken on the strength.	
			31/8/17. [illegible] Lieut. Comdg 97th Coy M.G.C.	

A5834 Wt. W4973/M687 750,000 8/16 D. D. & L. Ltd. Forms/C.2118/13.

ORIGINAL.

94th M. G. Coy.

WAR DIARY

FOR MONTH OF

SEPTEMBER 1917.

VOLUME XIV

Army Form C. 2118.

Instructions regarding War Diaries and Intelligence Summaries are contained in F. S. Regs., Part II. and the Staff Manual respectively. Title pages will be prepared in manuscript.

WAR DIARY
or
~~INTELLIGENCE SUMMARY.~~
(Erase heading not required.)

Place	Date	Hour	Summary of Events and Information	Remarks and references to Appendices
RIGHT SUB-SECTOR NIEUPORT SECTOR	1/9/17 -21/9/17		The Company was in the line in the S. GEORGES SubSector with 16 guns in the line, 14 on indirect S.O.S lines and 2 in the Front line.	[illegible]
COXYDE.	21/9/17		On the night 21/22nd the Company was relieved by the 14th M.G. Coy & proceeded to COXYDE.	[illegible]
BRAY-DUNES PLAGE	22/9/17 -24/9/17		The Company in billets at BRAY DUNES.	[illegible]
COXYDE	24/9/17 -29/9/17		On the 24th the Coy returned to COXYDE where it remained in Divisional Reserve till the 29th.	[illegible]
LEFT SUB-SECTOR NIEUPORT SECTOR	29/9/17 30/9/17.		On the night 29th/30th the Coy relieved 96th M.G. Coy. in the line in the LOMBARTZYDE Subsector.	[illegible]

A5834 Wt. W4973 M687 750,000 8/16 D. D. & L. Ltd. Forms/C.2118/13.

Army Form C. 2118.

Instructions regarding War Diaries and Intelligence Summaries are contained in F. S. Regs., Part II. and the Staff Manual respectively. Title pages will be prepared in manuscript.

WAR DIARY
or
~~INTELLIGENCE~~ SUMMARY.

(Erase heading not required.)

Place	Date	Hour	Summary of Events and Information	Remarks and references to Appendices
			During the month the following Casualties occurred –	
			1 O.R. Killed	
			1 O.R. Died of wounds	
			1 O.R. Wounded –	
			1 O.R. Evac. to C.C.S.	
			2/LT. F. MINTER and 2 O.R. were taken on the strength –	
			30/9/17 [signature] Lieut for O.C. 97th M.G. Coy.	[initials]

A5834 Wt. W4973 M687 750,000 8/16 D. D. & L. Ltd. Forms/C.2118/13.

Instructions regarding War Diaries and Intelligence Summaries are contained in F. S. Regs., Part II. and the Staff Manual respectively. Title pages will be prepared in manuscript.

WAR DIARY
or
~~INTELLIGENCE SUMMARY.~~
(Erase heading not required.)

Army Form C. 2118.

Place	Date	Hour	Summary of Events and Information	Remarks and references to Appendices
			During the month of October LIEUT. W. HANNAH proceeded to 123rd M.G. Coy as 2nd-in-Command on 20/10/17	
			LIEUT N.L.S. POWNALL proceeded to GRANTHAM on 13/10/17.	
			LIEUT P.G. HINGLEY reported from M.G. BASE DEPOT as Transport officer on 16/10/17.	
			1 N.C.O was wounded.	
			8 O.R. were evacuated to C.C.S & struck off strength.	
			3 O.R. reported from Base depot & taken on strength.	
			3 N.C.O's proceeded to England to join CADET UNIT & were struck off strength.	
			[illegible] Capt. Comdg. 97th M.G. Coy.	[illegible]

Army Form C. 2118.

Instructions regarding War Diaries and Intelligence Summaries are contained in F. S. Regs., Part II. and the Staff Manual respectively. Title pages will be prepared in manuscript.

WAR DIARY

or

~~INTELLIGENCE SUMMARY.~~

(Erase heading not required.)

Place	Date	Hour	Summary of Events and Information	Remarks and references to Appendices
LOMBARTZYDE SUBSECTOR	1/10/17 to 5/10/17.		The Company was in the line in the LOMBARTZYDE subsector NIEUPORT SECTOR –	[initials]
COXYDE	6/10/17 –		The Company was relieved by the 125th Coy M.G.C. on the night 5th/6th and marched to camp at COXYDE –	[initials]
UXEM	7/10/17 to 23/10/17		The Company marched to billets at UXEM on the 7/10/17 where it remained training till the 23/10/17 –	[initials]
RUBROUK	25/10/17 – 31/10/17		The Company left UXEM on the 23rd and marched to billets in RUBROUK area arriving on the 25th, where it remained training until 31st –	[initials]

ORIGINAL.

Vol 20

94th M.G. Coy.

WAR DIARY

FOR MONTH OF

OCTOBER 1917.

VOLUME XV

ORIGINAL

97th M. G. Coy.

WAR DIARY

FOR MONTH OF

NOVEMBER 1917

VOLUME XVI

Army Form C. 2118.

Instructions regarding War Diaries and Intelligence Summaries are contained in F. S. Regs., Part II. and the Staff Manual respectively. Title pages will be prepared in manuscript.

WAR DIARY
or
~~INTELLIGENCE SUMMARY.~~
(Erase heading not required.)

Place	Date	Hour	Summary of Events and Information	Remarks and references to Appendices
RUBRUCK	1.11.17		Total Strength of Company – 10 Off. & 253 other ranks (includ 61 att men) Company Parade 9 AM – Majority of Company re-inoculated in morning; remainder Barrage drill Route March – Football match played against the 2nd K.O.Y.L.I. in the afternoon. Result 2nd K.O.Y.L.I. 3 goals – Coy Team 1 goal. Weather, dull & damp. Casualties – Nil.	AWA
do	2.11.17		Work in the morning consisted of a Lecture by C.O.; Practice in methods of deploying; and Special Classes for N.C.O's in Compass Work & Map Reading, & Rangefinding. Casualties NIL. Majority of Company off duty owing to inoculation.	AWA
do	3.11.17		Training in the morning from 8.45 AM till 12.30 PM, including Special Classes as yesterday. After dark Nos 1 & 2 Sections took part in Brigade Scheme of assembling by night, using pack transport. Casualties NIL	AWA
do	4.11.17		Church Parade cancelled owing to wet weather – In afternoon, football match was played between 92nd Field ambulance & Coy. Result F.A. 5 Coy 2. Afternoon weather fine but cold – Casualties NIL.	AWA
do	5.11.17		10 gun team paraded at 7.30 as part of defending force in a Tactical Scheme against 2nd K.O.Y.L.I. – Remainder of Coy. carried out their usual training – In the afternoon the whole Coy. was put thro' Gas Test in Lachrymatory Gas – Weather fine – Casualties NIL.	AWA
do	~~6.11.17~~			

A5834 Wt. W4973/M687 750,000 8/16 D. D. & L. Ltd. Forms/C.2118/13.

Army Form C. 2118.

Instructions regarding War Diaries and Intelligence Summaries are contained in F. S. Regs., Part II. and the Staff Manual respectively. Title pages will be prepared in manuscript.

WAR DIARY
or
~~INTELLIGENCE SUMMARY.~~

(Erase heading not required.)

Place	Date	Hour	Summary of Events and Information	Remarks and references to Appendices
RUBRUCK.	6.11.17	.	Nos 1, 2, & 3 Section ½ No 4 Section paraded at 8 AM, taking part as defending force in Tactical Scheme with the 11th Border Regiment. Divisional Commander watched the Scheme visited the Barrage Battery of Nos 1 & 2 Sections. Weather fine – Casualties – NIL.	AMM
do	7.11.17		Very heavy rain in the morning cancelled Tactical Scheme with 16th H.L.I. & ~~remainder~~ of forenoon was spent in cleaning for inspection by Corps Commander. In the afternoon a football match was played against the 97th T.M.B's. Result Coy 4 – T.M.B's 0. (Divisional Tournament) Clear & sunny in afternoon. Casualties NIL.	AMM
do	8.11.17		Company with Transport paraded at 9.15 in Drill Order marched to Brigade Parade Ground for inspection which was carried out not by the Corps Commander but by the Divisional Commander. Weather very cold. Casualties NIL.	AMM
do	9.11.17.		Sections paraded under Section Officers the day was spent cleaning & getting ready to move. Casualties NIL. Special Classes for N.C.O's in Rangefinding & Map reading. Football Match Coy v 4th Coy Divisional Train was cancelled owing to the move. Weather wet.	AMM
Wormhoudt.	10.11.17		Company moved from RUBROUCK at 9.45 to billets near WORMHOUDT. Accomodation very limited & of indifferent quality. Heavy rain all day. Roads in very bad condition – Route via ARNEKE, LEDRINGHAM – WORMHOUDT. No stragglers. Units of the 2nd Division will billeted in & around WORMHOUDT. Divisional Commander passed the Brigade on the line of march. Casualties NIL.	AMM

A5834 Wt. W4973 M687 750,000 8/16 D. D. & L. Ltd. Forms/C.2118/13.

Instructions regarding War Diaries and Intelligence Summaries are contained in F. S. Regs., Part II. and the Staff Manual respectively. Title pages will be prepared in manuscript.

WAR DIARY
or
~~INTELLIGENCE SUMMARY.~~
(Erase heading not required.)

Army Form C. 2118.

Place	Date	Hour	Summary of Events and Information	Remarks and references to Appendices
ROAD CAMP Poperinghe.	11.11.17		Company paraded at 8.15 marched to ROAD CAMP via HAUTEKERQUE & WATOU arriving in Camp about 1.30 PM. Heavy traffic on the roads, & rain fell almost continuously. Cold was intense. Company were accomodated as follows Nos 1 & 2 Section Headquarters in Camp & Nos 3 & 4 sections in two farms on the outskirts of SAN JAN de BIEZEN. No stragglers altho' the march was difficult. Transport in open Standing near Camp. Casualties NIL	[illegible]
do	12.11.17		Sections paraded at 8.45 under section Officers at Transport lines for general cleaning of guns & stores. At 10.30 AM demonstration with Yukon packs was given. Remainder of day was devoted to the cleaning up of billets & kit. Weather damp & cold. Casualties NIL	[illegible]
do	14.11.17		Company bathed in the morning till 11.30 AM. 11.30 till 12.30 Close order Drill. The Company this day was organised into Batteries 'A' Battery (consisting of Nos 1 & 2 Sections) under Lieut G. Masters, "B" Battery (consisting of Nos 3 & 4 sections) under Lieut A M Humble. Lieut A M Humble proceeded on leave to U.K. Weather fine. Casualties NIL.	[illegible]
do	13.11.17		Company was inspected by C.O at 9 AM, remainder of morning being spent in Mob. training. Weather fine. Casualties NIL	
do	15.11.17		At 8.45 AM Nos 2, 3 & 4 Sections proceeded on Route March in Battle order. No 1 Section with limbers & pack transport practised carrying loads and methods of supplying ammunition on training area. Weather fine. Casualties NIL. The Brigade Major was present at training area	[illegible]

A5834 Wt. W4973/M687 750,000 8/16 D. D. & L. Ltd. Forms/C.2118/13.

Instructions regarding War Diaries and Intelligence Summaries are contained in F. S. Regs., Part II. and the Staff Manual respectively. Title pages will be prepared in manuscript.

WAR DIARY
or
~~INTELLIGENCE~~ SUMMARY.

(*Erase heading not required.*)

Army Form C. 2118.

Place	Date	Hour	Summary of Events and Information	Remarks and references to Appendices
ROAD CAMP POPERINGHE.	16/11/17		"A" Battery paraded at 8.15 and carried out practise with Yukon packs on Company training area. "B" Battery practised Barrage work – Casualties NIL	AWMA
do	17/11/17		Training was carried out as for yesterday in the morning. On the 15th Company played the 92nd Field Ambulance in the final of the Brigade Football Tournament "B". Result F.A 2. Company 1. — Casualties NIL.	AWMA
do	18/11/17		The morning was spent in delousing & disinfection of billets. Casualties NIL	AWMA
do	19/11/17		No 1 Section paraded with full battle kit & carried out demonstration on Training Area. Remainder of Company carried out training as follows: No 2 Section Rifle Practice on Range; "B" Battery Combined Drill & Gas Drill. In the afternoon a party of Officers & NCO's visited the raised map of the II Corps area at the Town Hall POPERINGHE Casualties NIL. Weather fine.	AWMA
do	20.11.17.		No 2 Section carried out training ~~with~~ on training area same as No 1 Section yesterday – No 1 Section Rifle practice. "B" Battery Barrage Drill Weather fine but dull — Casualties NIL	AWMA
do	21.11.17.		Company paraded in drill order at 9AM and ~~[illegible]~~ paraded with the Brigade at 10.15 when the Brigade was addressed by the Divisional Commander. Capt J. W. Gordon visited the forward area. – Casualties NIL.	AWMA
IRISH FARM	22.11.17		The Company proceeded to IRISH FARM by rail from RAILHOEK and was billeted in tents & huts – condition of the camp very bad, accomodation is very poor. Lieut W E Howard secured the billets, having been sent on the previous night for that purpose. The Company arrived in Camp about 2 PM. Casualties NIL.	AWMA

A5834 Wt. W4973 M687 750,000 8/16 D. D. & L. Ltd. Forms/C.2118/13.

Instructions regarding War Diaries and Intelligence Summaries are contained in F. S. Regs., Part II. and the Staff Manual respectively. Title pages will be prepared in manuscript.

WAR DIARY
or
~~INTELLIGENCE SUMMARY.~~
(Erase heading not required.)

Army Form C. 2118.

Place	Date	Hour	Summary of Events and Information	Remarks and references to Appendices
IRISH FARM.	23.11.17		Nos 3 & 4 Sections proceeded to the line together with 2 sections of 219th M.G. Coy. leaving Camp about 8.30 AM. These guns relieved guns of the 2nd, 3rd & 216th M.G. Coys. of the 1st Division, in a Battery position at YETTA HOUSES (D. 3. d. 6,6) Relief went smoothly and was complete by 10 AM. Weather misty — Casualties NIL.	AWM
do	24.11.17		Nos 1 & 2 Sections proceeded to the line leaving at 7 PM relieved guns of No 2 Coy. 1st Division. in positions at BELLEVUE RIDGE (D 5 c 4,8) (4 guns) & at WOLF FARM (D 4 b 20,08 & D 4 b 10.10 2 guns) & at WALLEMOLEN (D 3 b 80,62 & D 3 b 65 70 2 guns) Sect. H.Q. were at Pillbox at D 4 d. 85,80. — No 2 Sect H Q at D 4 a. 95.40. Relief was complete at 10.15 AM. Adv. Coy H.Q. were established at KANSAS FARM with Adv B.H.Q. Enemy shelling was rather below normal but increased in intensity in the evening. Casualties NIL. Rear Coy H.Q. went to CANAL BANK	AWM
CANAL BANK	25.11.17		Enemy's artillery activity was greater throughout the day and at 7 PM a heavy barrage was put down behind our front line. Our own S.O.S signal was put up, and about 8.30 PM fire gradually slackened. Our artillery barrage being very heavy & effective. Casualties 1 other rank killed. 1 gun destroyed by shell fire. Barrage battery fired continuously throughout the S.O.S. period. Enemy shelled duck board tracks throughout the night	AWM

Instructions regarding War Diaries and Intelligence Summaries are contained in F. S. Regs., Part II. and the Staff Manual respectively. Title pages will be prepared in manuscript.

WAR DIARY
or
INTELLIGENCE SUMMARY.
(Erase heading not required.)

Army Form C. 2118.

Place	Date	Hour	Summary of Events and Information	Remarks and references to Appendices
CANAL BANK	26.11.17.		Nos 1 & 2 sections carried out inter-team reliefs. Artillery activity remained above normal, & was particularly lively from dusk onwards. Weather bright & clear. Casualties 1 o.r. wounded.	AMA.
do	27.11.17.		Enemy's artillery very active throughout the day, all communications being heavily strafed and in the evening became very intense. Battery position was shelled with 5.9's & 77mm. heavily between 7PM - 8.30PM. & all gun positions appeared to receive attention. Carrying party with S.A.A. left KANSAS CROSS ROADS at 6.20 PM. & came in for heavy shelling in the vicinity of MEETCHELE. Casualties 2/LIEUT L.S.B. BROWN. (killed) Lieut M.C. DAVIDSON (wounded) Other ranks wounded 4.	AMA
do	28.11.17.		The Company was relieved by the 96th M.G. Coy. relief being complete by 12.30PM. Enemy's artillery again active. The company marched back to billets at CANAL BANK. Casualties 2/Lieut O.V. BARKER (killed) Other ranks wounded 4.	
do	29.11.17		Company moved from billets at CANAL BANK to IRISH FARM. The Coy. spent the day resting & a working party of 60 men & 2 Officers formed dumps for SAA at SOURCE FARM & BELLEVUE. Lieut A.M. Humble reported back from leave. Casualties NIL	AMA.
do	30.11.17.		The Coy. paraded at 10.45 & were inspected by C.O. The company bathed between 1 & 2 PM. and the afternoon was spent in cleaning up & preparing for the line.	

A5834 Wt. W4973 M687 750,000 8/16 D. D. & L. Ltd. Forms/C.2118/13.

Instructions regarding War Diaries and Intelligence Summaries are contained in F. S. Regs., Part II. and the Staff Manual respectively. Title pages will be prepared in manuscript.

WAR DIARY
or
~~INTELLIGENCE SUMMARY.~~

(Erase heading not required.)

Army Form C. 2118.

Place	Date	Hour	Summary of Events and Information	Remarks and references to Appendices
	30.11.17.		Increase in Strength during month — 1 O.R. from Hospital 4.11.17. 2 O.R. " Base Depot 7.11.17 1 O.R. " 2nd Bedfords. Total 4 Other Ranks	
			Decrease in Strength during month. 2 Off. 1 O.R. killed in action 1 " 7 " wounded " " 11 " evac. C.C.S. 12 " transferred to 219th Coy Total 3 Off 31 Other ranks.	[illegible]

WAR DIARY
or
~~INTELLIGENCE SUMMARY~~
(Erase heading not required.)

Army Form C. 2118. 1

Instructions regarding War Diaries and Intelligence Summaries are contained in F. S. Regs., Part II. and the Staff Manual respectively. Title Pages will be prepared in manuscript.

DECEMBER 1917.

97th Machine Gun Company

15

RECORD OFFICE No. RC/2950
2

Place	Date	Hour	Summary of Events and Information 321	Remarks and references to Appendices
[Iri]sh FARM	1.12.17		Strength of Company – 7 Officers and 220 O.R. (including 58 attached) The morning was spent preparing for the line, issuing operation orders &c. At 1PM. the Company left IRISH FARM by marched route for WURST FARM where they arrived about 4 o'clock. Limbers were used for transport of guns &c and mess packs as far as SPREE FARM. Route from SPREE FARM was by KANSAS HOUSE and No 6 TRACK. Company waited at WURST FARM until 8.30PM when Battalions began to pass up the tracks on their way to the assembly tapes. No 1 Section and No 2 Section fell in behind No 1 Battalion (2nd KOYLI) and followed them to VENTURE FARM where No 2 Section separated to join No 2 Batt. (16th H.L.I.) No 3 Section joined No 3 Batt (11th Borders) at WURST FARM and proceeded with them to the point of assembly. No 4 Section was similarly attached to Nos 4 & 5 Batt. (17th H.L.I. & 15 Lancs Fus) Objectives and dispositions were as shewn on attached map appended to copy of company operation order No 30. Except in the case of No 4 Section the assembly was carried out smoothly with the loss of only one casualty. While the troops were forming up artillery on both sides was exceptionally quiet and though the weather earlier in the night had been stormy with sleet showers, by midnight the wind had moderated, and the sky had cleared. The night was bright. Casualties 1 O.R. wounded.	Appendix "A" J.M.A.
do	2.12.17		Reports of completion of assembly were received about 12.30AM this morning with the exception of No 4 Section. Zero hour was at 1.55AM. when the assault began without artillery barrage. Rifle and machine gun fire from the enemy was encountered almost at once but did not lead to serious loss. Little opposition was met with, and at zero + 8 when the artillery	

22

Instructions regarding War Diaries and Intelligence Summaries are contained in F. S. Regs., Part II. and the Staff Manual respectively. Title Pages will be prepared in manuscript.

WAR DIARY
or
~~INTELLIGENCE SUMMARY~~
(Erase heading not required.)

Army Form C. 2118. (2)

DEC. 1917

9Y^th M. G. COMPANY

Place	Date	Hour	Summary of Events and Information 322	Remarks and references to Appendices
	2.12.17		and machine gun barrage came down, considerable ground had been gained. Enemy's artillery retaliation was feeble in front areas, but more intense towards the rear, on a line from Point 83 to MEETCHEELE. By 4.30 AM, the artillery activity had considerably subsided and the attack had checked on a line from V.28.b.42.30 to MALLET COPSE excluding VEAL COTTAGES thence in a south easterly direction to the front of VOX FARM and not including HILL 52. Communication from forward troops was very poor, only a few messages being received at Coy H.Q. At 8AM the position of the guns so far as could be ascertained were, roughly as follows:- 3 guns of No 4 Section in vicinity of V 29 a, 35.45; 3 guns of No. 3 section about V.23.d. 4.2; 1 gun of No 3 Section was at this time out of action in vicinity of VOCATION FARM; 1 gun of No 2 Section at V.30.a.35.60, 1 at V.30.a.52.60, 1 at approximately V.24.c.15.20, and the fourth gun just beside it. There was no trace of the guns of No 1 Section, 2 of which were known still to be in action with the Infantry on the extreme right of the Brigade front. The remainder of the day was extremely quiet and owing to the clear & sunny weather observation was good. Numerous parties of the enemy were seen moving behind their shell hole positions and particularly leading into WESTROOSEBEEK. A few snipers were active, but parties of stretcher bearers on both sides were allowed to move freely while collecting casualties. Artillery was very much below normal. Between 4.30 PM & 5PM, enemy artillery activity greatly increased, developing about 5PM into a regular barrage which preceded, enemy counter attack which appeared lately only to develop against the right flank of	

WAR DIARY
or
~~INTELLIGENCE SUMMARY~~
(Erase heading not required.)

Army Form C. 2118.

Instructions regarding War Diaries and Intelligence Summaries are contained in F. S. Regs., Part II. and the Staff Manual respectively. Title Pages will be prepared in manuscript.

DECEMBER 1917.
97 M. G. Coy

323

Place	Date	Hour	Summary of Events and Information	Remarks and references to Appendices
...SH FARM	2.12.17		the Brigade. By then all available guns having moved forward to the advanced positions held by the Infantry, and these came into action as soon as the attack developed. This enemy movement led to a withdrawal by all Battalions, which eventually took up a position practically on their original line. The machine guns having been left isolated in their forward positions withdrew later to conform with the general line. During the evening two gun teams particularly lost heavily, and two guns were put out of action. By 8PM the situation had again become clear, and 8 guns of the 96th M.G. Coy, were moved forward from their battery position to assist in the consolidation and close defence of the line in the vicinity of VIRILE FARM coming under direct orders of the G.O.C. 97th Infantry Brigade. The exact dispositions of the battalions at this time was very uncertain. Casualties 1 Officer wounded and at duty. 3 O.R. killed and 12 O.R. wounded. The weather was extremely cold.	
do.	3.12.17		The positions of the guns were definitely ascertained. The day was again quiet, but enemy snipers were particularly active especially in the neighbourhood of VOCATION and VIRILE FARMS where a number of casualties were caused. Orders were received about 4 PM. for the withdrawal of all guns of the Company on the relief of the Battalions in whose area they were that night. The time of this withdrawal was shortly afterwards altered to dusk, when gun teams were collected & proceeded to IRISH FARM. The day began bright and frosty, but became very cold at night. Hostile artillery was more active on our lines of communication at night. Casualties 1 O.R. killed, 8 O.R. wounded and 6 O.R. missing, three of which are presumed prisoners. Number of guns taken out of the line was 11.	SWMA

2449 Wt. W14957/M90 750,000 1/16 J.B.C. & A. Forms/C.2118/12.

Instructions regarding War Diaries and Intelligence Summaries are contained in F. S. Regs., Part II. and the Staff Manual respectively. Title Pages will be prepared in manuscript.

WAR DIARY
or
INTELLIGENCE SUMMARY
(Erase heading not required.)

Army Form C. 2118. 4.

DECEMBER 1917.
97th M G Coy.

324

Place	Date	Hour	Summary of Events and Information	Remarks and references to Appendices
IRISH FARM	3.12.17		During yesterday's operations a gun team of No 2 Section and neighbouring Infantry were much annoyed by an enemy machine gun, and two of the gun team succeeded in rushing the enemy post, and after bayonetting two of the gunners and scattering the remainder, brought in the gun intact.	
Dambre CAMP	4.12.17		The Company moved from IRISH FARM by train leaving about 10.5 AM – reached the new Camp about 11 o'clock. The last team of No 2 Section had reported from the line at IRISH FARM about 6.30 AM. The remainder of the day was spent in cleaning up – Casualties NIL. – Weather frosty.	
do	5.12.17		Kit and rifle inspection in the morning and the remainder of the day was spent in cleaning gun stores and limbers. Casualties NIL Weather dull and damp – 2/Lieuts T.C. MILLER and A.H. COLLINS reported for duty from the Base.	[initials]
do	6.12.17		The morning was spent in issuing clothing and necessary equipment; rifle inspection and limber fatigues – Casualties NIL. LIEUT A.N. HUMBLE appointed 2nd in Command of the Company vice LIEUT M C DAVIDSON wounded in action.	[initials]
do.	7.12.17		Part of the forenoon was spent in cleaning limbers &c and at 11.45 am the Brigadier addressed the Company. The afternoon was spent in Pay Parade and Baths. Weather wet. Casualties NIL	[initials]
do	8.12.17		The Company spent the day cleaning packs, equipment, limbers &c	[initials]
do	9.12.17		Church Parades in the forenoon. R.C.s at 9 AM – C of E at 10.15. Weather very wet and owing to this the afternoon parade was cancelled. Casualties NIL	[initials]

2449 Wt. W14957/M90 750,000 1/16 J.B.C. & A. Forms/C.2118/12.

Instructions regarding War Diaries and Intelligence Summaries are contained in F. S. Regs., Part II. and the Staff Manual respectively. Title Pages will be prepared in manuscript.

WAR DIARY
or
INTELLIGENCE SUMMARY
(Erase heading not required.)

Army Form C. 2118. (5)

DECEMBER 1917

94th M.G. Coy.

Place	Date	Hour	Summary of Events and Information	Remarks and references to Appendices
			325	
DAMBRE CAMP	10/12/17		Morning spent in usual inspections by Section Officers, followed by C.O's parade in full marching order and route march under section arrangements. In the afternoon limber parade and checking of section stores. L/Cpl. GALE left for A.A. course at II Corps School. At 2.30 p.m. four German 'planes flew over camp quite low, dropping bombs and literature at some little distance away. 11th Batt. Border Regt. came into camp last night. Casualties nil. Weather dull and damp, turning frosty towards evening. [initials]	
"	11/12/17		Limber parade & route march in morning. A reconnaissance of the lines of defence & communications in the new Divisional area was made by 2nd Lieuts. MINTER & MILLER. Very cold day. 6 o.r. reported as re-inforcements from 206th M.G. Coy. Casualties nil. [initials]	
"	12/12/17		Box respirator drill in morning, followed by drawing stores and care & cleaning. 2nd Lieuts. GARSIN & COLLINS, Sgt YATES & Cpl ROBERTSON carried out	

Instructions regarding War Diaries and Intelligence Summaries are contained in F. S. Regs., Part II. and the Staff Manual respectively. Title Pages will be prepared in manuscript.

WAR DIARY
or
~~INTELLIGENCE SUMMARY~~

(Erase heading not required.)

Army Form C. 2118.

DECEMBER 1917.

97th M.G. COMPANY.

326

Place	Date	Hour	Summary of Events and Information	Remarks and references to Appendices
DAMBRE CAMP	12/12/17		reconnaissance of new area included in Div. Area. Fitting of new containers for box respirators was begun and well pushed on. Coy Canteen was re-started. Weather frosty in morning & cold all day. Casualties NIL.	[illegible]
"	13/12/17		Usual inspections, close order & rifle drill, & route march in morning. Bathing in afternoon for whole company. Casualties NIL. Thick mist & very damp.	[illegible]
"	14/12/17		Whole company employed on putting bricks down on new horse standings just E of CANAL BANK. Work took all day and good progress was made. The bricks were got from YPRES. Weather damp & cold. 2nd Lieut. C.W. MAYOW reported for duty from Base & is taken on the strength. Casualties NIL	[illegible]
"	15/12/17		Whole company again employed on new horse standing. The bricking of the floor was completed and work was begun with the assistance of a party from 14th M.G. Coy. on a rec-	

2449 Wt. W14957/M90 750,000 1/16 J.B.C. & A. Forms/C.2118/12.

Instructions regarding War Diaries and Intelligence Summaries are contained in F. S. Regs., Part II. and the Staff Manual respectively. Title Pages will be prepared in manuscript.

WAR DIARY
or
~~INTELLIGENCE~~ SUMMARY
(Erase heading not required.)

Army Form C. 2118. (17)

DECEMBER 1917

97th M.G. COMPANY.

327

Place	Date	Hour	Summary of Events and Information	Remarks and references to Appendices
DAMBRE CAMP.	15/12/17		ons. Weather bright but cold. Casualties NIL.	
			Arrangements made with O.C. 96th M.G. Company for relief on 18th prox., his H.Q. being at HUBNER FARM (ref. POELCAPELLE SHEET 1/10,000).	
CANAL BANK	16/12/17		Company moved from DAMBRE CAMP to CANAL BANK (EAST), leaving camp at 1.30 p.m. Accomodation good and ample. Transport remained near ARRIVAL FARM. Work on horse standings was finished off with earth rammers. Casualties 1 O.R. accidentally wounded. Weather cold & clear, slight snow shower in afternoon.	
	17/12/17		Operation order for relief on 18th issued. Day was spent in preparing guns for the line, issuing rations, & supplies, etc. Wire received stating arrival at Div. Wing of 29 O.R. re-inforcements. Casualties NIL.	
HUBNER FM.	18/12/17		No. 1 Section left CANAL BANK at 7.30 a.m. to relieve guns of No. 96 M.G. Company at WINCHESTER & VON TIRPITZ FM's forming No. 3 Control Guides	

2449 Wt. W14957/M90 750,000 1/16 J.B.C. & A. Forms/C.2118/12.

Instructions regarding War Diaries and Intelligence Summaries are contained in F. S. Regs., Part II. and the Staff Manual respectively. Title Pages will be prepared in manuscript.

WAR DIARY
or
INTELLIGENCE SUMMARY

(Erase heading not required.)

Army Form C. 2118.

DECEMBER 1917

97th M.G. COMPANY.

328

Place	Date	Hour	Summary of Events and Information	Remarks and references to Appendices
HUBNER FM..	18/12/17		were met at GENOA FM. at 10 a.m. Route followed by whole company was via HAMMOND'S CORNER, CHEDDAR VILLA, CORNER COT & ALBERTA track. Nos. 2, 3, & 4 Sections left at 12.30 p.m., meeting guides at HUBNER FM. for No. 2 Control and at KRONPRINZ FM. for No. 1 Control. No. 2 Control was composed of No. 2 Section & half No. 4 Section & was disposed as follows:– 2 guns at BANFF HO., 2 guns at BURNS HOUSES, & 2 guns at VACHER FM.. No. 1 Control, with HQ at KRONPRINZ was composed of No. 3 Section & half No. 4 Section, disposed with 2 guns at TOURNANT FM., 2 guns in vicinity of PILL BOX 86 & 2 guns near VARLET FM.. Relief was complete at 7.30 p.m.. Teams were at the strength of 3 men with 1 N.C.O. for each pair of guns. Remainder of company moved to IRISH FM. in afternoon. Morning was foggy & misty. Enemy aircraft were active during the morning. Casualties NIL. [initials]	
	19/12/17.		Guns of No. 2 Control fired 4,000 rounds during night on CLEAR FM., SPIET ROAD and WESTWOOD HO.. Work was commenced on new shelter for guns at VARLET FM., but owing to severe frost, the ground was found very difficult to work. During previous 24 hours the enemy's artillery was very quiet & relief was reported to have gone smoothly. One of our machines fell in flames, during an air-fight, near battery positions on MOUSETRAP TRACK in front of CORNER COT.. Firing orders & range cards	

2449 Wt. W14957/M90 750,000 1/16 J.B.C. & A. Forms/C.2118/12.

Instructions regarding War Diaries and Intelligence Summaries are contained in F. S. Regs., Part II. and the Staff Manual respectively. Title Pages will be prepared in manuscript.

WAR DIARY
or
INTELLIGENCE SUMMARY
(Erase heading not required.)

Army Form C. 2118. 69.

DECEMBER 1917

97th M.G. COMPANY –

Place	Date	Hour	Summary of Events and Information 329.	Remarks and references to Appendices
HUBNER FM.	19/12/17		were issued to all Gun positions. 15 Boxes of S.A.A. were carried forward by No. 1 Control to TOURNANT FM. and PILL BOX 86 positions, five to the first & 10 to the second. Hot tea arrived at Adv. Coy. H.Q. at 2 a.m. & was then sent on to sections. Weather again very hard. Casualties. NIL.	[initials]
"	20/12/17		During previous 24 hours hostile artillery was quiet. The neighbourhood of VACHER FM. was slightly shelled with 77 mm. at intervals throughout the day. During the night hostile artillery was very much more active on our right & left flanks. E.A. activity was marked about 7 a.m. but from 9 a.m. onwards our own planes were much in evidence over the enemy's lines. A low-flying E.A. was attacked by one of our planes & driven down, grounding at V21 a. 50.50 (approx.). During the night WINCHESTER & VON TIRPITZ were bombarded with gas shells (mustard) but with only small effect. Work was carried on by No. 1 Control in getting up shelter-iron & other R.E. stores from KRONPRINZ DUMP to site of new shelter. Guns at BURNS HOUSES fired 4,000 rounds harassing fire. Casualties one O.R. wounded at IRISH FM. Hard frost continues.	[initials]
"	21/12/17		16 Boxes S.A.A. were carried forward by No. 2 Control to BANFF HO. During last night 4,000 were again fired by this control on definite tar-	

Instructions regarding War Diaries and Intelligence Summaries are contained in F. S. Regs., Part II. and the Staff Manual respectively. Title Pages will be prepared in manuscript.

WAR DIARY
or
INTELLIGENCE SUMMARY
(Erase heading not required.)

Army Form C. 2118.

DECEMBER 1917.

97th M.G. COMPANY –

330

Place	Date	Hour	Summary of Events and Information	Remarks and references to Appendices
[illegible]ENER FM.	21/12/17		Pits. No 1 Control got up all R.E. material from dumps & completed excavation. Emplacements at VACHER FM. were cut out & improved. All officers, excepting O.C. No 1 Control were relieved to-day, & as many men as possible. Previous 24 hours very quiet. Thick mist all day. Casualties one o.r. wounded at IRISH FM. Weather still very heavy.	[illegible]
" "	22/12/17		Enemy artillery was quiet throughout the day but showed activity from 8.30 p.m. to midnight. The WALLEMOLEN positions & track in vicinity got some heavy shells between 10.30 p.m. & 11 p.m., heavy shrapnel was put over the SLAB ROAD, yesterday. During the same period our own artillery was more marked, especially from 8 p.m. onwards, field batteries firing frequent bursts. Observation was very limited owing to thick mist during the whole of yesterday, but this cleared off after dark. Aerial activity nil. Casualties 1 o.r. killed & 1 o.r. wounded. Harassing fire was again continued on tracks, roads & DOUBLE COPSE.	[illegible]
" "	23/12/17		Very clear day & considerable artillery action on both sides yesterday. INCH HOUSES, BANFF HO, BURNS HOUSES & WINCHEST-	

Instructions regarding War Diaries and Intelligence Summaries are contained in F. S. Regs., Part II. and the Staff Manual respectively. Title Pages will be prepared in manuscript.

WAR DIARY
or
INTELLIGENCE SUMMARY
(Erase heading not required.)

Army Form C. 2118.

(11)

DECEMBER 1917

94th M. G. COMPANY.

331

Place	Date	Hour	Summary of Events and Information	Remarks and references to Appendices
	2[illegible]/12/17		Fm. were all shelled during the day. Visibility was high & several enemy aircraft crossed our lines flying very low about 7.30 a.m.. Our aeroplanes were also active. At 4.30 p.m. yesterday after considerable shelling in the direction of POELCAPPELLE the enemy opened a very heavy bombardment on our left & our S.O.S. rocket (two red & two white) were seen to go up. Artillery action was again normal about 5.30 p.m., though heavy shelling was then going on on our right flank. Our front remained quiet throughout the day. 4,000 rounds were again fired on given targets during previous 24 hours by guns of BURNS HQ. Shelter at WALLEMOLEN position is now about completed & two new ones have been commenced at the VACHER Fm. position. R.E. material being carried forward from YORK HQ. dump. All necessary material was got up last night. Casualties nil. [illegible signature]	

2449 Wt. W14957/M90 750,000 1/16 J.B.C. & A. Forms/C.2118/12.

WAR DIARY
or
~~INTELLIGENCE~~ SUMMARY.
(Erase heading not required.)

Instructions regarding War Diaries and Intelligence Summaries are contained in F. S. Regs., Part II. and the Staff Manual respectively. Title pages will be prepared in manuscript.

Army Form C. 2118.

DECEMBER 1917

94th M.G. COMPANY.

(12)

Place	Date	Hour	Summary of Events and Information	Remarks and references to Appendices
HUBNER FM	24/12/17		332 Operation Order No. 33 was issued at 1 a.m. on 23rd. Previous 24 hours very quiet. 4,000 rounds fired on harassing targets as per programme. There was a thick mist all yesterday & today, artillery activity was practically nil. Guides met two teams of 14th M.G. Coy. & 2 teams of 96th M.G. Coy. at GENDA FM. at 10.30 a.m. Remaining teams of 14th M.G. Coy. reached HUBNER and KRONPRINZ FMS. at 2 p.m. Relief went very smoothly with no shelling, & was complete at 6.30 p.m. The gun positions occupied by this company were as follows during the line.	

TOURNANT FM.	V 28 b. 35.10	VACHER FM.	V 26 d. 80.45
"	V 28 b 30.15	" "	V 26 d. 75.45
BANFF HQ.	V 24 b. 50.50	BURNS HOUSES	V 26 d. 51.49
" "	V 24 b. 45.60	" "	V 26 d. 45.50
PILL BOX 86	V 28 c. 78.60	WINCHESTER FM.	D 2 a. 25.60
" "	V 28 c. 80.89	"	D 2 a. 20.55
WALLEMOLEN	V 24 d. 80.10	VON TIRPITZ FM.	D 4 b. 45.68
"	V 24 d. 72.10	" "	D 4 b. 38.67

D. D. & L., London, E.C. (A8004) Wt. W1771/M2031 750,000 5/17 Sch. 52 Forms/C2118/14

(13)

Instructions regarding War Diaries and Intelligence Summaries are contained in F. S. Regs., Part II. and the Staff Manual respectively. Title pages will be prepared in manuscript.

WAR DIARY
or
INTELLIGENCE SUMMARY.
(Erase heading not required.)

DECEMBER 1917 — Army Form C. 2118.

97th M.G. COMPANY.

333

Place	Date	Hour	Summary of Events and Information	Remarks and references to Appendices
	24/12/17		Teams when relieved rendezvoused at CORNER COT whence H.Q. + Nos. 2 and 1 Controls proceeded by light railway to SIEGE CAMP. Rear Coy. H.Q. and No. 3 Control moved by road at 2 p.m. All were billetted in NISSEN HUTS. 27 O.R. reported for duty the night before last + are taken on the strength. Casualties Nil.	
SIEGE CAMP	25/12/17		CHRISTMAS DAY. Coy. parade at 12 NOON. Day spent in rest + cleaning up. Snow fell in heavy showers at intervals through-out the whole day + there was a bitter cold wind. Casualties Nil.	
	26/12/17		Company parade at 9 a.m. Remainder of morning spent in packing + cleaning limbers. Pay + foot parades in after-noon. S.O.S. message received at 8.50 p.m. ordering all units to prepare to move. Men to turn in but keep their boots on. Casualties 1 OR wounded. Operation Order for relief of Bde. by 86th Bde (29th Div.) on 29th inst. received.	

D. D. & L., London, E.C. (A8009) Wt W1771/M2031 750,000 5/17 Sch. 52 Forms/C2118/14

Instructions regarding War Diaries and Intelligence Summaries are contained in F. S. Regs., Part II. and the Staff Manual respectively. Title pages will be prepared in manuscript.

WAR DIARY
or
INTELLIGENCE SUMMARY.
(Erase heading not required.)

DECEMBER 1917. Army Form C. 2118.

97th M. G. COMPANY.

334

Place	Date	Hour	Summary of Events and Information	Remarks and references to Appendices
SIEGE CAMP	27.12.17		Capt Gordon proceeded to R.F.C. course at BERTANGLES. Company paraded at 9AM and the forenoon was spent cleaning and packing limbers and getting ready for the move. Casualties Nil	AWA.
do	28.12.17		Company paraded at 9AM. the day was spent cleaning up limbers and equipment. S.O.S. message recieved in the evening about 8.30 and the Company "stood to" for two hours when the message was cancelled. Orders regarding march of the Transport were cancelled at 9.30PM. Casualties NIL Weather very cold but bright	AWA.
do	29.12.17		A party of 2 Off + 50 men paraded at 7AM + proceeded by light railway to CORNER COT + the day was spent building dugouts near WINCHESTER. The remainder of the Company spent the day cleaning and packing. Orders were recieved at 9PM that owing to the non arrival of the relieving M.G. Company, the Company would not move to morrow. All orders for the move were therefore cancelled. Casualties NIL	AWA.

D. D. & L., London, E.C. (A8004) Wt W1771/M2031 750,000 5/17 Sch. 52 Forms/C2118/14.

(15)

Army Form C. 2118.

WAR DIARY
or
INTELLIGENCE SUMMARY.
(Erase heading not required.)

DECEMBER 1917.

97th M.G Company

Instructions regarding War Diaries and Intelligence Summaries are contained in F. S. Regs., Part II. and the Staff Manual respectively. Title pages will be prepared in manuscript.

Place	Date	Hour	Summary of Events and Information 335	Remarks and references to Appendices
SIEGE CAMP	30/12/17		The Company stood by from 8AM. and at 10AM. orders were received to carry on with orders already issued. The Company paraded at 10.30 & marched to ELVERDINGHE STATION. Dress. Full marching order with greatcoats worn. The transport left about 11.30 and marched to TUNNELLING CAMP. The Company arrived at the station about 11.30AM and entrained at 12.30. The journey to AUDRICK was a very cold one, and the Company arrived there about 6.30PM. Detraining was carried out very quickly and the Company marched off at 7PM and arrived at AUTINGUES about 9.30. A very heavy march owing to the snow. Billets were found at once, and after having a meal the men turned in. Casualties —— NIL.	[initials]
Autingues	31.12.17		The Company paraded at 10AM. and was inspected by the C.O. after which the men were dismissed and the remainder of the day was spent in cleaning equipment etc. Casualties NIL. Weather Bright and cold.	[initials]

D. D. & L., London, E.C. (A8094) Wt W1771/M2031 750,000 5/17 Sch. 52 Forms/C2118/14

CONFIDENTIAL

Vol 273

WAR DIARY

of

94th M.G. COMPANY –

From. 1st Jan 1918 To – 31st Jan. 1918.

JANUARY 1918 (1

Army Form C. 2118.

WAR DIARY
or
INTELLIGENCE SUMMARY. 97th M.G Coy.
(*Erase heading not required.*)

Instructions regarding War Diaries and Intelligence Summaries are contained in F. S. Regs., Part II. and the Staff Manual respectively. Title pages will be prepared in manuscript.

Place	Date	Hour	Summary of Events and Information	Remarks and references to Appendices
AUTINGUES	1.1.18.		The Company paraded at 10AM when it was inspected and addressed by the C.O. and then dismissed. Weather cold and bright Casualties NIL.	AMA
do	2.1.18.		Parade 9AM. 9 till 10AM Physical drill. 10.11 Squad drill with arms. 11.15 to 12.30 Cleaning and packing of limbers. In the afternoon a football match was played with the result Company 3. Brigade TMB 1. Weather bright and cold. Casualties — NIL. The C.O. returned from Course to-day	AMA
do	3.1.18		Brigade Holiday — There were no parades to-day. In the afternoon the Officers and Sergeants played the rest of company at football which resulted in a win for the Company by 4-3. In the evening a concert was held in the village estaminet. Lt. Gorsim returned from leave to U.K. Casualties — NIL.	AMA
do.	4.1.18.		The Company paraded at 9AM and the forenoon was spent as follows 9.10 Physical Training. 10.11 Squad Drill. 11.15 - 12.30 Machine gun drill. The afternoon was spent playing a football match between the Sections. Weather bright and clear.	AMA

(2)

JANUARY 1918 Army Form C. 2118.

Instructions regarding War Diaries and Intelligence Summaries are contained in F. S. Regs., Part II. and the Staff Manual respectively. Title pages will be prepared in manuscript.

WAR DIARY
or
INTELLIGENCE SUMMARY.
(Erase heading not required.)

97th Machine Gun Coy.

Place	Date	Hour	Summary of Events and Information	Remarks and references to Appendices
AUTINGUES	5.1.18.		The Company paraded at 9AM and the sections were inspected by the Section Officers. The forenoon was spent as follows:- 9-10 Company Drill and from 10-12.30 the sections were at the disposal of the section Officers. Capt Gordon proceeded on leave to UK. to-day. Weather, bright and clear but still cold. Casualties NIL	AUMA
do.	6.1.18.		Church Parade for RC's at 8.30AM but there was no C of E parade. All the men who have joined the Company (~~[illegible]~~ (a[illegible])) since 1.12.17 paraded at 11AM and were inspected by C.O. The Transport Section were also inspected at 11.30. In the afternoon a football match was played between the Company and the 2nd K.O.Y.L.I. A good match with the result 4-1 in favour of the K.O.Y.L.I. Casualties - NIL.	AUMA
do	7.1.18		The Company paraded at 9AM and the forenoon was spent as follows 9.15-10AM Physical Drill - 10-11 Company Drill 11-12.30 Gun cleaning and packing of limbers. The Company was inspected at 2PM by C.O. Football was played in the afternoon between the new Draft & the rest of Company. Lieut Shingley proceeded on leave.	AUMA

D. D. & L., London, E.C. (A8co4) Wt W1771/M2031 750,000 5/17 Sch. 52 Forms/C2118/14

(3)

Instructions regarding War Diaries and Intelligence Summaries are contained in F. S. Regs., Part II. and the Staff Manual respectively. Title pages will be prepared in manuscript.

WAR DIARY
or
INTELLIGENCE SUMMARY.
(Erase heading not required.)

JANUARY 1918.

Army Form C. 2118.

97th MACHINE GUN COY.

Place	Date	Hour	Summary of Events and Information	Remarks and references to Appendices
AUTINGUES.	8.1.18.		The Company paraded at 8AM for the Corps Commanders inspection at TOURNHEIM. Dress:- Drill order, Belts, Braces, Ammunition Pouches, Bayonets, Bayonet Scabbards, & Service Caps. Transport moved off at 7.45. The Company moved off at 8.30, & at that time the snow was coming down very heavily. At 9.10 a messenger was met on the road with orders that the parade was cancelled. The Company marched back to billets & the remainder of the forenoon was spent in cleaning up equipment and billets. Snow fell heavily in the afternoon. Casualties — NIL.	AMM
do	9.1.18.		The Company paraded at 9AM & the forenoon was spent in Physical Training, Gun & Squad Drill, & Limber cleaning. A football match had been arranged with the Brigade T.M.B. but owing to snow again falling heavily in the afternoon the match was cancelled. Casualties NIL.	AMM

D. D. & L., London, E.C.
(A8co4) Wt W1771/M2031 750,000 3/17 Sch. 52 Forms/C2118/14

JANUARY 1918. Army Form C. 2118. (4

WAR DIARY
or
~~INTELLIGENCE SUMMARY~~.
(Erase heading not required.)

Instructions regarding War Diaries and Intelligence Summaries are contained in F. S. Regs., Part II. and the Staff Manual respectively. Title pages will be prepared in manuscript.

97th MACHINE GUN COY.

Place	Date	Hour	Summary of Events and Information	Remarks and references to Appendices
AUTINGUES.	10.1.18		The Company paraded at 9AM & were inspected by Section Officers Dress – Full Marching Order – The remainder of the forenoon was spent in a route march till about 12.30. A foot inspection was held at 2.30. & the remainder of the day was spent resting – Weather clear & bright with a good fall of snow on the ground. Casualties – NIL.	AWMA
do	11.1.18		The Company paraded at 9AM and the forenoon was spent as follows: 9–10 Physical Training – 10–11AM Cleaning of limbers; 11.15–11.45 Anti-gas Drill. 11.45–12.30 Gun drill with gas masks. In the afternoon a lecture was given by an officer in the R.F.C. at TOURNHEM. 3 Officers and all the available NCO's attended this lecture. A football match was played between the Company and the 92nd Field Ambulance, which resulted in a win for the latter by 4.1 – Weather bright and clear – 2/Lieut C.W. MAYOW admitted to hospital to-day – Casualties NIL.	AWMA

D. D. & L., London, E.C.
(A8004) Wt W1771/M2031 750,000 5/17 Sch. 52 Forms/C2118/14

5

Instructions regarding War Diaries and Intelligence Summaries are contained in F. S. Regs., Part II. and the Staff Manual respectively. Title pages will be prepared in manuscript.

JANUARY 1918. Army Form C. 2118.

WAR DIARY
or
INTELLIGENCE SUMMARY.
(Erase heading not required.)

97th M.G. Company.

Place	Date	Hour	Summary of Events and Information	Remarks and references to Appendices
AUTINGUES	12.1.18		The Company paraded at 9AM. & were inspected by Section Officers. The forenoon was spent in Physical Training, Squad Drill, and cleaning and packing of limbers. The Company paraded again at 2.45 in full marching order and moved off at 3PM and marched to ZOUAFQUES where it arrived about 5.30PM. Billets were found at once & the men got settled down. The whole company with the exception of transport, is billeted in a big barn in the Village. Casualties NIL	amm
ZOUAFQUES	13.1.18		R.C's Church service was held at 10.15 in the village church. Nonconformist Service was held at TOURNEHEM at nine o'clock. The remainder of the company paraded at 10AM were inspected by the C.O and then dismissed. Weather wet & stormy — 15 O.R were transferred to the 219th M.G. Coy to-day — Casualties — NIL	amm

D. D. & L., London, E.C.
(A8003) Wt W1771/M2031 750,000 5/17 Sch. 52 Forms/C2118/14

Instructions regarding War Diaries and Intelligence Summaries are contained in F. S. Regs., Part II. and the Staff Manual respectively. Title pages will be prepared in manuscript.

WAR DIARY
or
~~INTELLIGENCE SUMMARY.~~
(Erase heading not required.)

JANUARY 1918. Army Form C. 2118.

94th M.G.Coy.

Place	Date	Hour	Summary of Events and Information	Remarks and references to Appendices
ZOUAFQUES	14.1.18	-	Nos. 2 + 3 Section paraded at 7AM and marched to the range at NORDLINGHEM where firing was carried out till 3PM. The practice consisted of firing at plates, each man firing 60 rounds among which were a number of stoppages – The other two sections spent the forenoon in physical training mechanism, gun cleaning &c – Weather, cold but bright Casualties — NIL	AMS
do.	15.1.18		Nos. 1 . 4 Section paraded at 7AM and marched to the range, but owing to the snow falling very heavily firing was postponed for the day, + the sections returned to billets about 11AM. The other two sections did the usual parades during the forenoon, but were confined to the billets on account of the weather. Gun cleaning, mechanism &c was carried on under the supervision of the Section officers – Casualties — NIL	AMS
do.	16.1.18		The days programme for firing was cancelled at 7AM by Brigade owing to the weather. The guns were taken to the section billets, + work in mechanism &c was carried out till 10.30, when the Brigadier came along + inspected	AMS

D. D. & L., London, E.C. (A8004) Wt W1771/M2031 750,000 5/17 Sch. 52 Forms/C2118/14

Instructions regarding War Diaries and Intelligence Summaries are contained in F. S. Regs., Part II. and the Staff Manual respectively. Title pages will be prepared in manuscript.

WAR DIARY
or
INTELLIGENCE SUMMARY.
(Erase heading not required.)

JANUARY. 1918 Army Form C. 2118. 7.

97th M.G. Coy

Place	Date	Hour	Summary of Events and Information	Remarks and references to Appendices
ZOUAFQUES	16.1.18		the Company in their Billets. The weather had cleared a little & Nos 2 & 3 Sections got the guns loaded on the limbers and marched to the Range at GUEMY. On arrival there the range was being used by the Infantry & the snow had started again. The "Cease Fire" was sounded about 12.15 and the Sections returned to billets. The remainder of the day was spent in the billets cleaning equipment &c. Casualties —— NIL.	[illegible]
do	17.1.18		The Company paraded at 9AM was inspected by C.O. Section Officers then took the men on parade ground, & the following programme was carried out. 9-10AM Physical Training, 10.11. Squad drill. 11-12.30 Gun cleaning & mechanism. The weather was wet in the afternoon & no recreational training was carried out. The Divisional Cross Country run which was to be held to-day, and for which five men of the Company had entered, was cancelled owing to the weather. Casualties NIL.	[illegible]

D. D. & L., London, E.C. (A8co4) Wt W1771/M2031 750,000 5/17 Sch. 52 Forms/C2118/14

(8

Instructions regarding War Diaries and Intelligence Summaries are contained in F. S. Regs., Part II. and the Staff Manual respectively. Title pages will be prepared in manuscript.

WAR DIARY
or
INTELLIGENCE SUMMARY.
(Erase heading not required.)

JANUARY 1918 Army Form C. 2118.

97th M.G. Coy.

Place	Date	Hour	Summary of Events and Information	Remarks and references to Appendices
NORDASQUES	18.1.18		Nos 2 + 3 Sections paraded at 7AM. and marched off to the range where field practices were carried out till three p.m. when the sections marched back to the new billets at NORDASQUES _ Nos 1 + 4 sections paraded at 9AM and spent one hour doing physical training; the rest of the forenoon being devoted to gun drill, packing limbers, + cleaning billets. Nos 1 + 4 sections paraded in full marching order at 12.30 and marched to NORDASQUES a distance of about 2 kilos. The afternoon was spent in the billets, with the exception of one fatigue party which cleaned up the limbers. The C.O. visited an R.F.C. Squadron at 10AM to day + spent the day there seeing the hangars, planes, guns &c. Casualties NIL. Weather clear but stormy.	AMA
do	19.1.18		The Company paraded at 9AM under the section-officers	

Instructions regarding War Diaries and Intelligence Summaries are contained in F. S. Regs., Part II. and the Staff Manual respectively. Title pages will be prepared in manuscript.

WAR DIARY
or
INTELLIGENCE SUMMARY.
(Erase heading not required.)

JANUARY 1918 (9)

Army Form C. 2118.

97th M.G. Coy.

Place	Date	Hour	Summary of Events and Information	Remarks and references to Appendices
NORD ASQUES	19.1.18		and one hour was spent in cleaning up equipment & the Company paraded again at 10.30 AM in drill order, with steel helmets and box respirators, marched to a field outside the Village, where the company was put through a gas test by the Divisional Gas Officer. The Company returned to billets about 1 PM. & the remainder of the day was spent resting. — The Transport of the Company along with all the other Transport of the Brigade moved off at 8.30 AM to-day to march to their first halting place — RUBRUCK. Casualties NIL. —— Weather dry, bright.	AMM
G" Camp	20.1.18		The Company paraded at full strength in full marching order at 4.15 AM & marched off at 4.30. Passed the starting point correct to time and arrived at AUDRICK at 6.30. Entrained at once, and the train pulled out at 7.10 AM and arrived at ELVERDINGHE where the Company detrained and marched to billets in G CAMP on the WOESTEN — POPERINGHE ROAD. — Casualties — NIL.	AMM

D. D. & L., London, E.C. (A8001) Wt. W1771/M2031 750,000 5/17 Sch. 52 Forms C2118/14

(10)

Army Form C. 2118.

Instructions regarding War Diaries and Intelligence Summaries are contained in F. S. Regs., Part II. and the Staff Manual respectively. Title pages will be prepared in manuscript.

WAR DIARY
or
INTELLIGENCE SUMMARY.
(Erase heading not required.)

JANUARY 1918.

97th M.G. Coy.

Place	Date	Hour	Summary of Events and Information	Remarks and references to Appendices
G. CAMP	21.1.18.		The Company paraded at 10AM and were inspected by the Acting C.O. The company was dismissed immediately after & the remainder of the day was spent resting. Capt Gordon returned from leave. — Casualties — NIL	
" "	22/1/18		Small kit inspection & work on limbers in morning. Baths in afternoon under 2nd Lieut. MAYOW. Heavy rain in morning until 9a.m. when it became sunny, but rain again fell about 4.30 p.m. 2nd Lieut. MINTER proceeded on leave to U.K.	[initials]
" "	23/1/18.		Company under section officers for P.T., anti-aircraft instruction, care & cleaning of guns. Mild clear day. Our aircraft busy at night bomb-dropping. Casualties nil.	[initials]
" "	24/1/18		Company in morning carried out P.T. & cleaning & packing of limbers. C.O. inspected harness and equipment of transport. Orders received for move to-morrow, about 8.30 p.m. Bright & mild. Casualties nil.	[initials]

D. D. & L., London, E.C. (A8001) Wt. W1771/M2031 750,000 5/17 Sch. 52 Forms/C2118/14

11

Army Form C. 2118.

WAR DIARY
or
~~INTELLIGENCE~~ SUMMARY.

(Erase heading not required.)

JANUARY 1918.

97th M.G. Company.

Instructions regarding War Diaries and Intelligence Summaries are contained in F. S. Regs., Part II. and the Staff Manual respectively. Title pages will be prepared in manuscript.

Place	Date	Hour	Summary of Events and Information	Remarks and references to Appendices
CYRILLE VAN DAMME	25/1/18.		Morning spent in cleaning up of camp & packing for move. 2nd Lieut. H. GARSIN admitted to hospital suffering from P.U.O. 2nd Lieut. T.C. MILLER did the billeting. Marched out of camp at 12.30 p.m. & arrived in new billets about 2 p.m. Company is in Dug-outs & 1 NISSEN HUT at CYRILLE VAN DAMME with officers & H.Q. in farm house. No. 4 Section in WOESTEN. 2nd Lieut. MAYOW & 4 o.r. went up to reconnoitre the line starting from "G" camp at 7 a.m. Fine spring-like day. Casualties NIL.	
"	26/1/18		C.O's conference at Bde. H.Q. at 10.30 a.m. Lieut. A.H. HUMBLE went up the line to the H.Q. of 1st M.G. Coy. to reconnoitre & arrange details of relief. Miller & 5 o.r. also went up to reconnoitre the line. Collins & party of 34 o.r. left at 8.30 a.m. for working party under RE's at J2 BRIDGE on CANAL. Remainder of company were employed in construction of latrines, roofing & screening & put a new NISSEN hut well in hand. O.O. No. 34 issued for relief. Very thick mist & colder. Casualties NIL.	

D. D. & L., London, E.C. (A8001) Wt. W1771/M2031 750,000 5/17 Sch. 52 Forms C2118/14

Instructions regarding War Diaries and Intelligence Summaries are contained in F. S. Regs., Part II. and the Staff Manual respectively. Title pages will be prepared in manuscript.

WAR DIARY
or
~~INTELLIGENCE SUMMARY.~~
(Erase heading not required.)

JANUARY 1918.

97th M. G. Company.

Army Form C. 2118.

Place	Date	Hour	Summary of Events and Information	Remarks and references to Appendices
CYRILLE VAN DAMME	27/1/18		C.O. went up line to H.Q. of No 1 M.G. Coy. One man per gun team (14) was sent up to the line to take over fire orders, etc. leaving at 2.30 p.m. under 2nd Lieut. COLLINS who went up to see the positions he will actually be taking over. 2nd Lieut MAYOW went up also to see his positions. Company at physical training & gun work in morning. Work on new NISSEN hut was continued all day. Misty & much colder. Casualties Nil.	[illegible]
MONDOVI WOOD	28/1/18		Morning spent in issuing rations, socks, etc. to men going into the line, packing of stores & blankets for Q.M. stores at Transport Lines. Billeting & advance party from No 1 M.G. Coy arrived in morning & took over accomodation in camp & area stores. Sections, Coy. H.Q. and rear Coy H.Q. under C.S.M. marched out at 2.30 p.m. Guides were picked up at 4.45 p.m. at LANCIER + ROADS. Transport was taken as far up as point U.8 d.08.80 (Sheet A1 1/10,000). Relief was complete	

D. D. & L., London, E.C.
(A8001) Wt. W1771/M2031 750,000 5/17 Sch. 52 Forms/C2118/14

Instructions regarding War Diaries and Intelligence Summaries are contained in F. S. Regs., Part II. and the Staff Manual respectively. Title pages will be prepared in manuscript.

WAR DIARY
or
~~INTELLIGENCE SUMMARY.~~
(Erase heading not required.)

JANUARY 1918

99th M. G. Company.

Army Form C. 2118.

Place	Date	Hour	Summary of Events and Information	Remarks and references to Appendices
MONDOVI WOOD	28/1/18		at 7.30 p.m., & was carried out very smoothly. Casualties Nil. Frosty & bright moon at night. F.W.G.	
"	29/1/18		Retaliatory fire was carried out by No. 3 sections Gun at LONELY MILL last night for activity of enemy M.G. firing at HILL 20. All emplacements seem in good order, drainage being the principal work to be carried out. Gun positions are all, with the exception of FAIDHERBE Gun in a closed emplacement, in the nature of built up breast-works. Guns are divided into 3 groups:- No 1 - Guns at HILL 20 (2) and FAIDHERBE (1) under 2nd Lieut. COLLINS with H.Q. on HILL 20. No. 2. Guns at LONELY MILL (2) and MANGELARE (2) under 2nd Lieut. MAYOW with H.Q. at MORTIER POST. No. 3. Guns at CATINAT, ISLANDE, & PAPEGOED POSTS (2 each) and VICTORY FARM (1) in Belgian area. Work was commenced on new dug-out for Gun at VICTORY. D.M.G.O. came to Coy. H.Q. in morning with O.C. 29th M.G. Coy. Very quiet day. Frosty. Casualties 1 O.R. accidentally wounded. F.W.G.	

D. D. & L., London, E.C. (A8071) Wt. W1771/M2031 750,000 5/17 Sch. 52 Forms C2118/14

Instructions regarding War Diaries and Intelligence Summaries are contained in F. S. Regs., Part II. and the Staff Manual respectively. Title pages will be prepared in manuscript.

14.

Army Form C. 2118.

WAR DIARY
or
INTELLIGENCE SUMMARY.
(Erase heading not required.)

JANUARY 1918

97th M.G. Company

Place	Date	Hour	Summary of Events and Information	Remarks and references to Appendices
MONDOVI WOOD	30/1/18		Alternative position for left gun at LONELY MILL was commenced, and sand-bagging & thickening of walls of nearly all emplacements carried out. Revetting was begun at HILL 20 positions. Most positions are under direct observation, movement has to be very slight during the day, & all work done after dark. Guns on HILL 20 & at LONELY MILL fired 300 rounds in retaliation for enemy m.g. fire. The new dug-out for gun in area of 4th Belgian Div. was completed last night & latrine constructed with duck-board tracks. Order boards renewed at all positions. Casualties Nil.	[illegible]
"	31/1/18.		O.C. 14th M.G. Company came in in morning to arrange details of relief, & went round guns of Nos. 2 & 3 Groups with O.C. Coy. Foggy & cold morning. Alternative emplacement at LONELY MILL completed & the others widened. New road cut to alternative positions at MANGELARE, improvements to H.Q. at MORTIER carried out. Casualties Nil. MONDOVI WOOD lightly shelled with 5.9's yesterday. Quiet day to-day. Strength of company 11 Officers. 238 Other Ranks.	

D. D. & L., London, E.C. (A8001) Wt. W1771/M2031 750,000 5/17 Sch. 52 Forms C2118/14

CONFIDENTIAL

Vol 24

WAR DIARY

OF

94th M. G. COMPANY

FOR PERIOD - 1st FEBRUARY TO 21st FEBRUARY 1918

(15.

Army Form C. 2118.

Instructions regarding War Diaries and Intelligence Summaries are contained in F. S. Regs., Part II. and the Staff Manual respectively. Title pages will be prepared in manuscript.

WAR DIARY
or
~~INTELLIGENCE SUMMARY.~~
(Erase heading not required.)

February 1918

97th. M.G. Coy

Place	Date	Hour	Summary of Events and Information	Remarks and references to Appendices
MONDOVI WOOD	1/2/18		Work at HILL 20 POST has been pushed on well. Men were instructed carefully in the dispositions of the infantry and action in case of attack. T.O. reported at Coy. H.Q. in afternoon and received instructions for relief to-morrow. Operation orders were issued for relief, and instructions issued. Very quiet day, foggy and frosty. Casualties NIL. Various R.E. stores sent up at night.	APPENDIX "A" [initials]
ASTOR CAMP.	2/2/18		Very quiet day. Guides for 14th Company came down to Coy H.Q. at 4.30 p.m. when O.C. 14th Company also arrived to take over. Relief was reported complete at 6.30 p.m and went very smoothly. Company billeted in AMBROSE CAMP with officers quarters and H.Q. at ASTOR CAMP. Bright sunny day with cold wind. Casualties NIL.	[initials]
" "	3/2/18		Company bathed in morning at ELVERDINGHE under 2nd Lieut COLLINS. D.M.G.O. called in afternoon, & spoke of new organisation for M.G. Companies. Day was spent in general cleaning up and rest. Fresh & sunny. Casualties NIL.	[initials]
" "	4/2/18		Company under Section officers for gun work in morning. O.C. proceeded to line to arrange details of relief with 14th M.G. Coy.	

D. D. & L., London, E.C. (A8031) Wt. W1771/M2031 750,000 5/17 Sch. 52 Forms C2118/14

(16)

Army Form C. 2118.

WAR DIARY
or
~~INTELLIGENCE SUMMARY.~~
(Erase heading not required.)

FEBRUARY 1918.

97th M. G. COMPANY.

Instructions regarding War Diaries and Intelligence Summaries are contained in F. S. Regs., Part II. and the Staff Manual respectively. Title pages will be prepared in manuscript.

Place	Date	Hour	Summary of Events and Information	Remarks and references to Appendices
ASTOR CAMP	4/2/18		Operation orders for relief brought out in afternoon. Cold & clear day. Casualties NIL.	APPENDIX "B" [initials]
MONDOVI WOOD	5/2/18		O.C. went to Bde. H.Q. at BRISSEIN ~~House~~ FARM at 8 a.m. to arrange transfer of attached men of 17th H.L.I to 16 H.L.I. as the 17th Battn. is being broken up as is happening in all brigades which are being reduced to 3 battalions only. Company left AMBROSE CAMP at 1.30 p.m. Guides were met at MONDOVI WOOD (Coy. H.Q.). Relief was reported complete at 6.30 p.m. and again went very smoothly. There was slight rifle fire at night and also M.G. fire – apparently patrol encounters. AJAX FARM was shelled with a few 5.9's during the night; otherwise all quiet. Lieut. W.E. HOWARD reports his arrival at POPERINGHE from FLEXICOURT by wire. Casualties NIL.	[initials]
"	6/2/18		Drainage scheme outlined for HILL 20 position. Improvements (internal fittings and traverse walls outside) at Coy. H.Q. put well in hand. 2nd Lieut. MAYOW not at all well. Major Lothian, at	

D. D. & L., London, E.C. (A8001) Wt. W1771/M2031 750,000 5/17 Sch. 52 Forms/C2118/14

(117)

Instructions regarding War Diaries and Intelligence Summaries are contained in F. S. Regs., Part II. and the Staff Manual respectively. Title pages will be prepared in manuscript.

WAR DIARY
or
INTELLIGENCE SUMMARY.
(Erase heading not required.)

FEBRUARY 1918.

97th M. G. COMPANY.

Army Form C. 2118.

Place	Date	Hour	Summary of Events and Information	Remarks and references to Appendices
MONDOVI WOOD	6/2/18		present commanding 11th Border Regt. called in at Coy. H.Q. about 2 p.m. and the Bde. Major at 3 p.m. Casualties NIL. Quiet day.	[initials]
"	7/2/18		Material for new shelter for gun teams at CATINAT POST was drawn from CORMORAN DUMP in the morning and after being run up on the trolley line to MONDOVI was carried forward from there, a certain amount being sent up while it was still daylight. Remainder of material was got up at dusk. Site for new shelter was selected early in morning, having been necessitated by the institution of No. 1 Battalion's H.Q. at CATINAT POST. Work was begun on new shelter at 9 p.m. and it was completed and floored by 3 a.m. on 8th. Boche put over a good deal of shrapnel during the day intermittently - mostly high "woolly" stuff. Very dark & stormy night with driving showers of cold rain. Casualties NIL.	[initials]
"	8/2/18		Officer of 96th Company came in in morning to arrange details for relieving guns of the company at FAIDHERBE (2), HILL 20 (2),	

D. D. & L., London, E.C.
(A8001) Wt. W1771/M2031 750,000 5/17 Sch. 52 Forms/C2118/14

Instructions regarding War Diaries and Intelligence Summaries are contained in F. S. Regs., Part II. and the Staff Manual respectively. Title pages will be prepared in manuscript.

WAR DIARY

~~or~~

~~INTELLIGENCE~~ ~~SUMMARY.~~

(Erase heading not required.)

FEBRUARY 1918.

Army Form C. 2118.

97th M. G. Company.

Place	Date	Hour	Summary of Events and Information	Remarks and references to Appendices
MONDOVI WOOD.	8/2/18		LONELY MILL (2) and MANGELARE (1). Quiet day. Clear but dull. Casualties NIL.	
"	9/2/18.		Drainage work at nearly all positions is being carried on, and new buttress at Coy. H.Q. being built. When pulling down old wall a box containing two new belt drums for the Boche light M.G. was unearthed, filled with S.A.A. 2nd Lieut. MINTER reported in evening with rations from leave. Quiet day. Casualties NIL.	
"	10/2/18		2nd Lieut. MINTER relieved 2nd Lieut. COLLINS at HILL 20 this morning. Duck board track is being laid to VICTORY POST. Sandbag revetment at HILL 20 completed and officer's dug-out enlarged & entrance renovated & widened. Casualties NIL.	
"	11/2/18.		Lieut. ELDER came in to arrange details of relief of four of his guns in the Corps Line by this company. Major Lothian of 11th Borders brought in Lieut. Col. Beazley their new C.O. Positions at FAIDHERBE, HILL 20, LONELY MILL and MANGELARE were relieved this evening by 96th Coy. Capt. WILLIAMS, 96th M.G. Coy	

D. D. & L., London, E.C. (A8001) Wt. W1771/M2031 750,000 5/17 Sch. 52 Forms/C2118/14

(19.

Instructions regarding War Diaries and Intelligence Summaries are contained in F. S. Regs., Part II. and the Staff Manual respectively. Title pages will be prepared in manuscript.

WAR DIARY
~~or~~
~~INTELLIGENCE~~ SUMMARY.
(Erase heading not required.)

FEBRUARY 1918. Army Form C. 2118.

97th M. G. COMPANY.

Place	Date	Hour	Summary of Events and Information	Remarks and references to Appendices
MONDOVI WOOD	11/2/18		Spent night at Coy. H.Q., unable to find H.Q. for himself. Very quiet night. Relieved teams of Nos. 4 & 3 sections to CHEVAL FARM. [initials]	
"	12/2/18		Extremely quiet day. Work at Coy. H.Q. was proceeded with rapidly & is being well done. Casualties Nil. [initials]	
"	13/2/18		Very quiet day. Operation orders for relief ~~of~~ 219th Company's guns in the Corps Line with four of ours were brought out. Emplacement at MANGELARE was strengthened and men's shelters at ISLANDE erected & camouflaged. Duck-board floors were put in. Casualties Nil. [initials]	
"	14/2/18		No. 4 Section came in to relieve four guns of 219th Coy. at U8d. 70.60, U8d.90.55. - U8a 55.55. U7b.00.55. Relief was very smooth and was reported complete at 6.48 p.m. No. 3 Section relieved No. 2 Section at PAPEGOED and ISLANDE. ~~Ablutions~~ ~~[illegible]~~ Work at Coy. H.Q. was completed. Casualties Nil. [initials]	APPENDIX "~~B~~C".
"	15/2/18		At 3.40 a.m. an artillery strafe was opened on the Belgian front & word was received that an enemy raid was in progress.	

D. D. & L., London, E.C. (A8001) Wt. W1771/M2031 750,000 5/17 Sch. 52 Forms C2118/14

Instructions regarding War Diaries and Intelligence Summaries are contained in F. S. Regs., Part II. and the Staff Manual respectively. Title pages will be prepared in manuscript.

(26.

WAR DIARY
or
~~INTELLIGENCE SUMMARY.~~

(*Erase heading not required.*)

FEBRUARY 1918.

Army Form C. 2118.

97th M.G. COMPANY.

Place	Date	Hour	Summary of Events and Information	Remarks and references to Appendices
MONDOVI WOOD	15/2/18		Bde. Major rang up ordering as many guns as possible to switch round and open fire on Belgian front. Calculations were made out and the guns at PAPEGOED, ISLANDE and CATINAT opened fire in about an hour. Remainder of day quiet on the whole. Alternative position at VICTORY POST was commenced & R.E. material carried up. Casualties NIL.	
"	16/2/18		Quiet day: a certain amount of shrapnel being sent over. Very fine weather. New position at VICTORY POST completed. Casualties Nil.	
"	17/2/18		Calculations & arrangements made for participation in coming raid by 96th and 97th Brigades. Ammunition brought up and distributed. Lieut. Col. J. Reade, the newly appointed C.O. of Divl. M.G. Battalion called in about 7.30 p.m., checked calculations and then went round guns. Very quiet day & night. Casualties NIL.	
"	18/2/18		Operation orders for raid were issued late last night. O.C.	APPENDIX "D"

D. D. & L., London, E.C.
(A8001) Wt. W1771/M2031 750,000 5/17 Sch. 52 Forms C2118/14

Instructions regarding War Diaries and Intelligence Summaries are contained in F. S. Regs., Part II. and the Staff Manual respectively. Title pages will be prepared in manuscript.

WAR DIARY
~~or~~
~~INTELLIGENCE SUMMARY.~~
(Erase heading not required.)

FEBRUARY 1918.

97th M.G. COMPANY.

Army Form C. 2118.

Place	Date	Hour	Summary of Events and Information	Remarks and references to Appendices
MONDOVI WOOD	18/2/18		14th M.G. Coy. came in to arrange details of relief. Very fine day. All guns were ready to open fire by 7.30 p.m. Zero hour was at 11 p.m. Raid very successful. Artillery & Stokes Mortar barrage reported very effective. First Batch of prisoners came in to CATINAT POST about 12.15 a.m. (19th). Enemy retaliation very feeble. Fine day. Guns fired well (12 in all from this company). Casualties Nil.	
"	19/2/18		Operation Order No. 42 was brought out for relief and instructions issued. Very quiet day. S.A.A. and R.E. material for a battery position were got up at night. 97th Bde. were relieved by 14th Inf. Bde. to-night. Casualties Nil.	APPENDIX "E"
"	20/2/18		Company was relieved and proceeded to BOESINGHE CAMP where No. 2 Section & Rear Coy. H.Q. had moved earlier in the day. Relief was complete about 7.30 p.m. and billets reached at 10.30 p.m. when men had a hot meal. Billets comfortable. Casualties Nil	
"	21/2/18		Rest & cleaning up. FORMATION OF M.G. BATTALION	

H. Gordon Capt.
Comdt. 97th M.G. Coy.

APPENDIX "A"

97th Machine Gun Company.

Operation Order No 35.

SECRET. Copy No..1...

Refce A1. 1/10,000.
BIXSCHOOTE. - 1/10,000.
BELGIUM. 28 N.W. - 1/20,000.

1. The 14th Machine Gun Company will relieve the 97th Machine Gun Company in the HET SAS sector on the night 2nd/3rd February 1918.

2. Guides. One guide per gun from No 1 Control, (4 guns) and No 2 Control (4 guns) will be at Company H.Q. U.1.d. No. 30. at 4.30. pm. whence they will guide incoming teams straight to their positions. One guide per gun from No 3 Control, (4 guns) will be on the road at CATINAT POST at 4.30 p.m. where they will pick up the incoming teams.

3. Personnel of Rear H.Q. will move off from their billets on the CANAL BANK at 3.45 p.m. + move direct to AMBROSE CAMP.

4. Handing Over. (a) Receipts for all tripods, belt-boxes, trench + area stores, R.E. Material etc. will be obtained, three copies being retained by out-going teams. All lists should be very carefully compiled + receipts should be show where the stores actually are.

(b) The same procedure will be carried out by the C.S.M. at rear Coy. H.Q. but tripods + belt boxes will not be handed over.

(c) In addition to petrol tins for carrying water for drinking purposes, two petrol tins will be handed over filled with water for use in the gun, a each gun position

(d) All Officers will hand over Company Defence Orders, programme of work in hand, and work still to be done, + will explain same to incoming officers. Range cards and

Sheet 4.

Fire orders boards will be handed over at each position + incoming teams shown the position of S.A.A. reserves.

5. Transport. One limber to move rear Coy H.Q. stores will be at rear Coy H.Q. at 4.0 p.m. The C.S.M. will arrange for a loading party for this limber, + 4 men to accompany it, and unload at AMBROSE CAMP.
One limber will be at point U.8.d.04.70. at 4.30 p.m. for H.Q. + cook's stores. Transport Officer will arrange for to have this limber unloaded at AMBROSE CAMP.
Three limbers, (one per control) will be at point U.8.d.04.70 at 5.45.p.m. to pick up guns etc:- of out-going teams.

6. Reports of relief complete will be made by runners to Company H.Q., the following code being employed:-

Relief Complete. - MONSTROUS.

7. On completion of relief teams will proceed to AMBROSE CAMP. B.10.d.

8. ACKNOWLEDGE.

Issued at 8 p.m.

[signature] Capt.
Comdg 97th M.G. Compy.

Copies to:-
No. 1. C.C.
" 2. 2nd in Command.
" 3. C.C. No 1 Control
" 4. " " 2 "
" 5. " " 3 "
" 6. O.C. No 14 M.G. Coy.
" 7. H.Q. 97th Infy Bde.
" 8. D.M.G.O.
" 9. Transport Officer.
" 10. C.S.M.
" 11. War Diary.
12. File.

APPENDIX "B"

97th Machine Gun Coy Operation Order No 37.

SECRET. Copy No. 12.

Reference:- A.1. 1/10,000
BIXSCHOOTE. 1/10,000.

1. The 96th M.G. Coy will relieve the 97th M.G. Coy at the undermentioned positions in No.1 Brigade Area on the night 11/12th February 1918.

U.6.d.50.40. and U.6.d.45.40.		FAIDHERBE.
U.5.c.40.20. and U.5.c.30.25		HILL 20.
U.10.a.50.60.	(Right gun)	MANGELARE.
U.10.b.45.10 and U.10.b.40.10.		LONELY MILL.

2. Guides. One guide found by Company H.Q. will meet incoming teams at CHARPENTIER CROSS Rds at 2.45 p.m. One guide for FAIDHERBE, one guide for HILL 20, one guide for MANGELARE and one guide for LONELY MILL, will be sent to Company H.Q. from these positions, & will rendezvous there not later than 3.15 p.m. on the 11th inst. They will guide teams from Company H.Q. to their respective positions by the shortest possible route.

3. Handing Over. Great care must be taken in handing over all fire orders, lines of fire, range cards, orders for sentries etc. The usual lists of Trench Stores, S.A.A. & maps will be made out & receipts obtained in duplicate, one copy being forwarded to Company H.Q. together with reports of relief complete. Belt boxes and tripods will be handed over at all gun positions.

4. Transport. One G.S. Limbered wagon will be at LANCIER CROSS ROADS at 5.30 pm, to pick up guns & spare parts of the down outgoing teams.

5. Destination of teams on completion of relief will be notified later.

6. Reports of relief complete will be made to Company H.Q. U.8.d.40.30, by runner, the following code being employed.

Relief Complete.	RELIABLE.
Heavy Shelling.	VERY.
No Heavy Shelling.	MAN.

7. ACKNOWLEDGE.

[illegible signature]
Capt
Commanding 97th M.G. Co.

10th Febry 1918.

Issued at 8.40. p.m.

Copies to:-

1. O.C.
2. 2nd in Command.
3. O.C. No 1 Control.
4. O.C. No 2 "
5. O.C. No 3 "
6. O.C. 96 M.G. Coy.
7. H.Q. 97 Infy Bde.
8. D.M.G.O.
9. Transport Officer.
10. C.S.M.
11. War Diary.
12. [illegible]

APPENDIX "C"

99th Machine Gun Coy. Operation Order No 39.

SECRET.

Copy No. 11

Reference :- A1. 1/10,000.
BIXSCHOOTE. 1/10,000.

1. No 4 Section, ~~[illegible]~~ 99th M.G. Coy. will relieve 4 guns of the 219th M.G. Coy. on the night 14/15 Febry. 1918, at positions in the Corps Line, as follows:- U.8.d.70.60 - U.8.d.90.55. - U.8.a.55.60 - U.7.b.00.55.

2. Guides. One guide for the guns at U.8.d.70.60, and U.8.d.90.55, one guide for the gun at U.8.a.55.55, & one guide for the gun at U.7.b.00.55, will be met at LANCIER CROSS ROADS at 3 p.m. on the 14th inst.

3. Transport. One limbered wagon will be available for transport of guns, tripods etc.:-

4. Handing Over. Guns & tripods will be taken in to the new positions, but 14 belt-boxes per gun will be handed over at each emplacement by 219 Coy. M.G.C. Receipts for these and all other trench stores, including Order Boards, Range Cards, & maps, will be made out in duplicate, one copy being forwarded with Report of relief complete to Company H.Q. at U.8.d.40.30.

5. Report of relief complete will be made by runner, the following code being employed:-

Relief Complete. REINFORCEMENTS.

6. ACKNOWLEDGE.

[signature]
Capt.
Commanding 99th M.G. Coy.

13th Febry. 1918.
Issued at 3.0. p.m.

Copies to:-
No. 1. O.C.
2. 2nd in Command.
3. O.C. No 4 Section
4. Lt ELDER. 219 M.G. Coy.
5. O.C. 219 M.G. Coy.
6. H.Q. 99th Brigade
7. D.M.G.O.
8. Transport Officer
9. C.S.M.
10. War Diary
11. File

APPENDIX "D"

97th Machine Gun Company.

Operation Order No 40.

SECRET.

Copy No..10...

Reference Maps. A.1. 1/10,000.
BIXSCHOOTE. 1/10,000.

1. Information. The 96th & 97th Infantry Brigades will carry out raids on enemy positions on the night 18/19th Feby 1918, as under:-

96th Infantry Brigade. Area O.35.d.1.0. to U.4.b.8.4.

97th Infantry Brigade.
Right Attack. On area bounded on the South East by the road running N.E. through U.4.b. & on the North by a line running parallel to that road from U.4.a.88.30. to U.4.b.45.60.
Centre Attack. SURCOUFF FARM pill boxes.
Left Attack. Posts about U.3.b.45.55.

2. Intention (a) Securing identifications.
(b) Killing, capturing, or permanently injuring as many of the enemy as possible.

3. Troops allotted. (a) Right attack, 3 Officers & 60 men of the XI Border Regt.
(b) Centre attack. 1 Coy. 2nd K.O.Y.L.I.
(c) Left attack 1 Coy. ...Do....
Artillery, machine guns, and trench mortars will co-operate.

4. Hour of Zero Zero hour will be notified later.

5. Assembly. The raiding parties will take up positions close in rear of our outpost line, at zero – 30 minutes, & will be in their positions of assembly by zero – 15 minutes.

6. Action of Artillery At zero, an intense artillery bombardment will open on all objectives. At zero + 28 mins: artillery will slacken off, & at zero + 48 mins artillery fire will cease.

7. Action of Machine Guns.
(a) All guns of the 97th M.G. Coy will, at zero, put down a standing barrage on a line running from O.34.b.05.20 to O.35.a.20.40, & will continue firing until zero + 30 minutes, when they will cease fire, & stand by for

(9)

Instructions regarding War Diaries and Intelligence Summaries are contained in F. S. Regs., Part II. and the Staff Manual respectively. Title pages will be prepared in manuscript.

WAR DIARY
or
INTELLIGENCE SUMMARY.
(Erase heading not required.)

JANUARY 1918.

97th M.G. Coy.

Army Form C. 2118.

Place	Date	Hour	Summary of Events and Information	Remarks and references to Appendices
NORD ASQUES	19.1.18		and and hour was spent in cleaning up equipment ~~to~~ the Company paraded again at 10.30 AM in drill order, with steel helmets and box respirators, marched to a field outside the Village, where the company was put through a gas test by the Divisional Gas Officer. The Company returned to billets about 1 PM. & the remainder of the day was spent resting. — The Transport of the Company along with all the other Transport of the Brigade moved off at 8.30 AM to-day to march to their first halting place – RUBRUCK. Casualties NIL. —— Weather dry, bright.	AMM
G" Camp	20.1.18		The Company paraded at full strength in full marching order at 4.15 AM & marched off at 4.30. Passed the starting point correct to time and arrived at AUDRICK at 6.30. Entrained at once, and the train pulled out at 7.10 AM and arrived at ELVERDINGHE where the Company detrained and marched to billets in G CAMP on the WOESTEN – POPERINGHE ROAD. — Casualties – NIL.	AMM

D. D. & L., London, E.C. (A8001) Wt. W1771/M2031 750,000 5/17 Sch. 52 Forms C2118/14

(8

Instructions regarding War Diaries and Intelligence Summaries are contained in F. S. Regs., Part II. and the Staff Manual respectively. Title pages will be prepared in manuscript.

WAR DIARY
or
INTELLIGENCE SUMMARY.
(Erase heading not required.)

JANUARY 1918 Army Form C. 2118.

97th M.G. Coy.

Place	Date	Hour	Summary of Events and Information	Remarks and references to Appendices
NORDASQUES	18.1.18		Nos 2 + 3 Sections paraded at 7AM. and marched off to the range where field practices were carried out till three p.m, when the sections marched back to the new billets at NORDASQUES _ Nos 1 + 4 sections paraded at 9AM and spent one hour doing physical training; the rest of the forenoon being devoted to gun drill, packing limbers, + cleaning billets. Nos 1 + 4 sections paraded in full marching order at 12.30 and marched to NORDASQUES a distance of about 2 kilos. The afternoon was spent in the billets, with the exception of one fatigue party which cleaned up the limbers. The C.O. visited an R.F.C. Squadron at 10AM to day, + spent the day there seeing the hangars, planes, guns &c. — Casualties NIL. Weather clear but stormy.	AMA
do	19.1.18		The Company paraded at 9AM under the section officers	

D. D. & L., London, E.C. (A8004) Wt W1771/M2031 750,000 3/17 Sch. 52 Forms/C2118/14

30 minutes, ready to open fire immediately on the same barrage line, in response to any S.O.S. signal.

(b) Detailed firing instructions are shewn on Appendix "A".

(c) The gun of No 4 Section at U.7.b.90.60, will move up on the morning of the 18th inst into position beside the gun at U.8.a.35.53.
All guns will be in position by zero – 1 hour.

(d) Belt boxes of each gun emplacement will be made up to 20 per gun, & "T" Bases, & "T" aiming marks will be employed. Every care will be taken to prevent short shooting, & depression stops used under the barrel casing in all cases. All guns will fire through screens to conceal flash, but auxiliary aiming marks must be made easily visible for checking direction.

(e). At zero + 60 minutes all guns will return to their normal positions, & lay on their usual night lines.

8. Synchronization of Watches. Watches will be synchronized at No 1 Battalion H.Q. on 18th Febry. O.C. No 1 Control will take two watches for synchronization at the above hour.

9. Communications.

(a) Company H.Q. will be in telephone communication with H.Q. of 96 M.G. Coy at CRAONNE FARM.

(b) A runner's post will be established by the Company at U.9.c.5.3.

10. ACKNOWLEDGE.

18th Febry. 1918

Issued at 7.30 a.m.

Copies to:- 1. O.C.
2. 2nd in Command.
3. 2/Lt F. MINTER.
4. 2/Lt. A.H. COLLINS.
5. 2/Lt C.W. MAYOW.
6. 97th Infy Brigade
7. O.C. 33rd Bn. M.G.C.
8. 96th M.G. Coy.
9. 219th " "
10. War Diary
11. [illegible]

APPENDIX 'E'

97th Machine Gun Company Operation Order No 41.

SECRET.

Copy No....1....

Reference Maps. A1. 1/10000
BIXSCHOOTE 1/10,000
SHEET 28 NW. 1/20,000

19th February 1918.

1. The 14th Machine Gun Company will relieve the 97th Machine Gun Company in the left sub sector of the Divisional Front on the night 20/21th February 1918.

2. Guides One guide from each of the following positions will report at Company H.Q. not later than 5.30 p.m on the 20th inst. MANGELARE. CATINAT. BLANDE. PAPEGOED. VICTORY. D.1. F.1. & F.2. Incoming teams will be met at Company H.Q. & guided thence by the shortest possible route to their respective gun positions.

3. Handing Over. All tripods & 14 Belt Boxes per gun will be handed over in addition to the usual trench stores. Lists of maps, orders, order boards, range cards, defence orders etc:- will be carefully compiled in duplicate and receipts obtained, one copy being sent to Company H.Q. together with report of relief complete.

4. Signallers will be prepared to hand over at 4 p.m on 20th & the whole of H.Q. personnel, with the exception of two runners, will move off from Company H.Q. at 5.50 p.m.

5. Transport. Two G.S. limbered wagons will be at MONDOVI DUMP at 4.15 p.m. one for the guns of No 2 Control & the other for No 1 Control & No 4 Section.
One limber for H.Q. will be at MONDOVI DUMP at 5.30 p.m & after loading, will proceed with H.Q. personnel.

6. Teams of each control will rendezvous at MONDOVI DUMP & march off under their respective Officers.
A hot meal will be prepared for these teams on their arrival in camp.

7. Reports of relief complete will be made by runners to Company H.Q. as under.
Relief complete GRATIFYING.

8. On completion of relief teams will proceed to DEKORT CAMP. B.3.c.2.6. Orders for advance party have been issued seperately.

9. ACKNOWLEDGE.

[signature]
....CAPT.,
Comdg. 97th M. G. Coy.

19th Febry 1918.

Issued at 1.30 p.m.

Copies to:- No 1. O.C.
2. 2nd in Command.
3. 2/Lt F. MINTER.
4. 2/Lt. C. MAYOW.
5. 2/Lt. A. COLLINS.
6. O.C. 14 M.G. Coy.
No 7. H.Q. 97th Brigade
8. O.C. [illegible] M.G. Batt
9. Transport Officer.
10. C.S.M.
11. War Diary
12. File

O P E R A T I O N O R D E R S
14TH COMPANY MACHINE GUN CORPS. NO.43.

Copy No. 6

Ref maps. A.1. 1/10,000.
BIXSCHOOTE. 1/10,000.
BELGIUM. 28.N.W. 1/20,000.

1. The 14th Machine Gun Company will relieve the 97th Machine Gun Company in the Left Sector of the Divisional Front on the night of the 20/21st February, 1918.

2. Positions will be taken over as follows:- (by sections).

1. Gun	VICTORY	"C" Section under 2/Lieut. S.V.Spear.
2. Guns	PAPEGOED	
2 Guns	ISLANDE	
2. Guns	CATINET	"A" Section under 2/Lieut. E.H.Dallas.
1. Gun	MANGELARE	
4. Guns	CORPS LINE	"D" Section under 2/Lieut. W.
D1, D2, F1, F2.		Sharrock and 2/Lieut. A.J.Wilder.

"B" Section will be in reserve .
HdQrs will proceed to the line with "D" Section.

3. Guides for all guns will be at Company Headquarters (MANDOVI WOOD) at 6.p.m.

4. 1 N.C.O, per gun will proceed to the line 24 hours in advance. Guides to take them to their respective positions will be at 97th M.G.Coy's HdQrs MANDOVI WOOD at 4.p.m, on the 19th instant.

5. Sections will move off at the following times:

"C" Sections	3.50.p.m.
"A" Section.	4. p.m.
"D" Section & HdQrs.	4.10.p.m.

6. Tripods, belt-boxes, S.A.A., etc, will be taken over at the gun positions from the 97th M.G.Company together with all firing instructions, Retaliation Schemes, Order Boards, Maps and Programme of work in hand. Receipts for these, and all other Trench Stores will be exchanged, two copies being retained by incoming Sections. These receipts will be forwarded to Coy HdQrs by first runner on day following relief.

7. Strength of Gun Detachments will be 1 N.C.O, and 4 men. A roll by teams will be sent to Coy HdQrs by Section Officers by 12 noon 21st instant.

8. 24 Hours rations will be carried by all ranks into the line.

/Completion.

9. Completion of relief will be reported to Coy HdQrs by runner in code words as follows:-

RELIEF COMPLETE...............WIND.
NO UNUSUAL SHELLING...........CUSHY.
UNUSUAL SHELLING..............UP.

10. Company HdQrs will be at MANDOVI WOOD, (U.8.d.40.30.)

11. ACKNOWLEDGE.

W. Harrison Captain,

19.2.18. Comdg, 14th Coy Machine Gun Corps.

Copies to:-

No. 1. O.C.
No. 2. O.C. "A" Section.
No. 3. O.C. "B" "
No. 4. O.C. "C" "
No. 5. O.C. "D" "
No. 6. O.C. 97th M.G.Coy.
No. 7. H.Q. 14th Inf Bde.
No. 8. O.C. 32nd Div. M.G. Batt.
No. 9. Transport Officer.
No. 10. C.S.M.
No. 11. War Diary.
No. 12. File.

[illegible] "A" to accompany 97th. Inf. B[illegible]

Date.	Unit.	From.	To.	Relieved by:-	[illegible] rendezvous [illegible]	[illegible]	Remarks.
Feb. 191[illegible] 19th.	97th. Inf. Bde.	? ISSEIN FARM.	WOESTEN.	14th. Inf. Bde. Head Qrs.	-	-	-
19th.	11th. Border. Regt.	Reserve. CANAL BANK. etc.	VAN DAMME CAMP. (B.1.d.	2nd. Dorsets.	[illegible] ROADS. meeting 2nd DORSETS. at (CAN[illegible] RDS. at [illegible]. am.)		[illegible] a.m. Guides will take advance parties to camp. Unit will go (train from [illegible] X ROADS, - details later.
19th.	2nd. K.O. [illegible] L.I.	Line-Left subsector.	REMINGHOF [illegible] FARM CAMP. S.24.a.0[illegible].0[illegible].	?/8th. Royal Scots.	[illegible] X ROADS. (All particulars later. For routes "In" and "Out." see Table "B")	9.30.p.m. By train from CHA[illegible] X ROADS,	
19th.	16th. High. L.I.	Support. (Left Sub-sector.)	BABOONCAMP. B.3.b.	1?th. High. L.I.	CHARPENTIER X ROADS.	6.30.p.m. Will march to their Camp. 16th. High. L.I. will be transferred from 97th. Inf. Bde. at 12 noon on the 20th inst. and will become 32nd. Div. Pioneer Batt. - For routes "In" and "Out" see Table "B".	
19th.	97th. T.M.B.	Line.	WOESTEN.	14th. T.M.B.	All details to be arranged between Commanding Officers concerned.		
20th.	97th. M.G. Coy.	Line.	DEKORT. Camp (B.3.c.8.8.)	14th. M.G.C.			

-10.-

NOTE:- (i) Guides will consist of 1 man per Batt. H.Q. 1 per Coy. [illegible] 1 per Platoon.
(ii) Usual distances will be observed on the march in accordance with Fourth Army No. G.S. 148. 100' between Platoons East of Canal.

Table "A" to accompany 97th. Inf. Bde. O.O. 204.

R O U T E S.

Guides will take relieving Units by the following Routes:-

FORWARD SYSTEM.
Right Coy. Batt.
in Forward System.

Company coming in.
By Road via LANCIER X ROADS - HOUDOVI DUMP - BRIDGE of ALLEN,
(U.8.d.9.8.) (U.[illegible].c.9.8.)
thence along Track through HOUDOVI WOOD, past [illegible] (U.[illegible].d.[illegible].30)
up track to HOUCHARD POST.
Company coming out.
By track across [illegible] BRIDGE (U.8.d.45.30) - BALL BRIDGE (U.14.a.8.3.)
Track past GRENADIER FARM (U.13.d.93.30.) - KORTEKEER CABT. (U.13.d.95.70)
LANCIER X ROADS - CHARPENTIER X ROADS.

Centre
Coy.

Company coming in. CHARPENTIER X ROADS - LANCIER X ROADS - NEW YORK -
CARRET DE LONDRES to where CATINAT Track crosses Road U.8.a.3.9. -
CATINAT POST up Track to [illegible] POST.
Company coming out. Follow the same route down to CHARPENTIER X ROADS.

Left
Coy.

Company coming in. CHARPENTIER X ROADS - LANCIER X ROADS. (U.13.d.1.3.) -
NEW YORK - (U.13.b.70.35.) - CARRET de LONDRES. (U.8.b.7.4.) -
ISLANDE POST - [illegible] POST.
Company coming out. [illegible] POST - ISLANDE POST - thence by MANGIN
Track - BOCHE X ROADS (U.24.d.35.80.) - CHARPENTIER X ROADS -
T.24.c.80.37.)

Support
Coy.

Company coming in. - CHARPENTIER X ROADS - LANCIER X ROADS -
CARRET de LONDRES. - ISLANDE POST.
Company coming out. - ISLANDE POST via MANGIN TRACK to BOCHE
X ROADS - CHARPENTIER X ROADS.

Support
Battalion.

Coys. at MANSHOEK and GOURBI FARM will use MANGIN TRACK.
Coys. at CHAUNE FARM and [illegible] WOOD will march by Road.

7. The completion of Reliefs which will be reported by wire and runner to Brigade Head Quarters as under:- *(The Commander of the Sector will pass on)*

Relief complete ... LEAVE.
Heavy shelling ... SHORT.
No heavy shelling ... LONG.

8. The relief of the Anti-Aircraft Guns will take place as under:-

Relief of A.A. guns in Forward Area and of Left Sub-sector by 14th. Inf. Bde. will take place on the 19th. February.

A guide for each gun in 97th. Bde. Area will be at CHARPENTIER X ROADS, 8.a.m. 19th. February to meet one man per gun from the 14th. Inf. Bde. coming up to take over gun position etc.

The Units of the 97th. Inf. Bde. will be responsible for the Anti-Aircraft defence during the 19th. inst. until relieved by the gun teams of the 14th. Inf. Bde. which will come up with their Units on the night 19th. February.

The representatives of the 14th. Inf. Bde. will have with them a paper showing to which gun they are posted.

9. Advance parties from Units of 14th. Inf. Bde. consisting of:-

1 Officer per Company.
1 N.C.O. per platoon.
1 Runner per Company.
1 Lewis Gunner per *Team*
1 Signaller per Company.

will arrive at CHARPENTIER X ROADS at 8.a.m. on the morning of the 19th. inst. and remain in the Line until the arrival of their Units.

Guides should be at CHARPENTIER X ROADS to meet these parties coming up to this point by train at 8.a.m. and take them up to Battalion Head Quarters.

10: Brigade Head Quarters will close at BRISSTIN HOUSE after relief, and re-open at WOESTEN.

11: A C K N O W L E D G E.

[signature] Captain,
for Brigade Major,
97th. Inf. Bde.

Issued at *3-15 pm*

to:-
1. G.O.C.
2. Brigade Major.
3. Staff Capt.
4. 11th. Border Regt.
5. 2nd. K.O.Y.L.I.
6. 16th. High. L.I.
7. 97th. M.G.Co.
8. 97th. T.M.Bty.
9. 32nd. Division.
10. -do.-
11. 14th. Inf. Bde.
12. 96th. Inf. Bde.
13. 97th. Bde. Signals.
14. No. 4 Co. Div. Train.
15. Supply Officer.
16. Area Com. WOESTEN.
17. War Diary.
18. -do.-
19. File.

[illegible]

Copy No. 7
19th.Feb.1918.

97th.Infantry Bde.Operation Order No.204.

1. The 14th.Infantry Brigade will relieve the 97th.Inf. Bde. in the Left Subsector of the Divisional Front on the night of the 19th./20th.February, in accordance with the attached Table "A".

2. All other details regarding the relief will be arranged between Commanding Officers concerned.

3. The greatest care is to be taken to hand over all Posts now held by this Brigade and to ensure that the relieving Units receive full details regarding the maintenance of connection in the Outpost Line.

The Officer Commanding a Post will not leave it until he is satisfied that the relieving Officer knows the position and extent of all the Defences of the Post, the position of and means of communication with adjoining posts, Company and Battalion Head Quarters, the orders for the Defence of the Post, and all other information concerning the command which he is taking over.

4. All A.A.Mountings, Defence Schemes, Maps, Schemes of Work, Work in progress and all other information about the Line will be taken over on relief.

5. Instructions regarding Advance Parties are being issued separately.

Advance Parties will take over with the greatest care, all Parade, Bombing and Football Grounds, Ranges and Bayonet and Bullet Courses, and obtain the agreements as to use made with owners for these.

They will also obtain a list of Ammunition and Material handed over, and forward it to Brigade Head Quarters.

6. The 14th.Machine Gun Coy. will relieve the 97th. Machine Gun Coy. in the Left Sub-sector of the Divisional Front on the night of 20th./21st.February.

All details of relief to be arranged between Commanding Officers concerned.

O.C.97th.M.G.Coy. will detail one O.R. to remain behind at each position until incoming detachments are satisfied that they know their lines of fire, and are acquainted with all orders.

/7.

www.ingramcontent.com/pod-product-compliance
Lightning Source LLC
Chambersburg PA
CBHW080852230426
43662CB00013B/2080
* 9 7 8 1 4 7 4 5 1 6 3 9 6 *